STICKING IT OUT

STICKING IT OUT

From Juilliard to the Orchestra Pit,
a Percussionist's Memoir

PATTI NIEMI

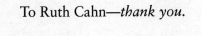

To Ruth Cahn—*thank you.*

Few parents would fall to their knees and pray that their daughter becomes a drummer. They might hope for a violinist or flute player, but it's the rare parent who secretly longs for a girl who beats on drums. If a ten-year-old drops this bomb as a career path, it's a safe bet that it is *her* dream.

What was desirable for my parents, however, was having a kid with a goal. We all want that — a passion, a path, a destination so clear that it makes getting up in the morning easy. My goal was to play percussion in an orchestra. That focus provided a pleasure that eased the dread of crawling out of bed to get to rehearsal before school, which in upstate New York meant it was still dark outside and below freezing. It made practicing after school easy even though that meant forgoing TV with — in those days — all four of its channels.

I started along this path on one of those bitter March mornings. Instrument lessons were still part of the public school curriculum in 1975, and my class was marched to the auditorium for a music aptitude test. Afterward, I waited for the letter to arrive that would tell my parents that my scores had averaged above the 65th percentile and I should be encouraged to begin learning a musical instrument. The letter never arrived.

Somehow, however, I had determined that there was no better way to stand out than to engage in sanctioned banging, and I was undeterred. We lined up to hand the band director our forms — girl after girl choosing flute, boy after boy choosing drums — and when the director saw that I'd specified "drums," he told me I had chosen well. It turned out that the aptitude test had been divided into two parts, "rhythm" and "melody." I'd scored in the 99th percentile for rhythm and the *first* percentile for melody. "You probably just misunderstood the instructions for the melody part," the band director said kindly. I had not. The test results were a sign that I had chosen the correct instrument.

That was only the beginning. What started as a 30-minute group lesson once a week quickly blossomed: private lessons, band, school orchestra, community youth orchestra, solo competitions, summer music camp, classes for music history and theory, recitals, concerts, practicing, and more practicing. I had to have parents who would pay for all of it and tolerate the endless banging coming from my room.

Most important, I had to *want* it. Gratification — winning an audition to play in an orchestra — would be long delayed, if it came at all. I understood by the time I was in high school that I could practice for years and still not get a job because there were too many of us who wanted to play in orchestras and too few orchestras for us to play in. I had to be willing to go through the audition process — show up with 70 or 80 of my peers for one job opening and take my turn behind a screen for five terrifying minutes of playing, while a committee of musicians sat on the other side of the screen, judging me.

By the time I finished high school, I had been pursuing my goal for eight years. It was time to go to a conservatory. I wanted to be in a big city, surrounded by classical music; I needed good teachers and good colleagues. I found all of that at a school whose storied name even non-musicians would recognize.

Now the real competition would begin.

1
. . . there was practicing.

For those of us who began in the fall of 1983, our formal introduction to Juilliard took place in the school's recital hall on a soggy September morning. Onstage was acting president Gideon Waldrop, standing in for last year's president, Peter Mennin, who had recently dropped dead. This, to paraphrase, was our orientation:

Whether it's playing music, acting, or dancing, you are what you do. We don't care about your private life. Make the school look good.

Welcome to Juilliard. Now go practice.

And practice I did — relentlessly, persistently. Quantity mattered; there was no time to waste. For all the practicing I would do over the years, I never went at it as desperately as I did those first few weeks at Juilliard.

It would be reasonable to guess that getting accepted to Juilliard might make me relax for a while. I could walk the hallowed halls with their orange wallpaper and think, *I'm attending the most famous music school in the world. This is where I will learn how to win an audition.*

Reasonable, but wrong. My thoughts were about math: there were about 50 orchestras in the country in which one could earn a living, three or four percussionists per orchestra, and, at any given audition, about 75 others like me who would show up for one opening. I waited with my fellow vultures around the country for death or retirement to make room for us.

The truth was, most of the students I'd been sitting with at orientation would not get jobs in music. We were beginning a long, winnowing process — those who ran out of time, money, stamina, or courage would fall by the roadside. This knowledge filled me with a creeping dread. I was a walking piece of anxiety-filled meat, and the only offensive against that fear was to practice.

So I practiced. Unlike music itself, there was no romance here — learning to play an instrument was the point at which art collided with sport. You had to be comfortable with solitary confinement and endless, mind-numbing repetition. Imagine an uninitiated apartment dweller hearing that a violinist is moving in next door. He might be expecting beautiful music to accompany life's mundane activities, maybe a nice Bach sonata while washing the dishes. What he'll get instead is scales, three octaves up and three back down, major then minor, slowly, and then arpeggios, followed by some technical études. Just about the time the neighbor is ready to open the window and leap to his death, the musician might finally begin learning one of those beautiful Bach sonatas, excruciatingly slowly, with missteps for weeks before it becomes a polished product. Next day, start again with the scales.

Finding a place to practice was a sport all its own. There were 20 other drummers crowding the halls with me that fall — too many for the number of available jobs *or* practice rooms. We had only two studios dedicated to us: big windowless rooms anchoring each end of our hallway and filled with the odd tools of a percussionist's trade: xylophones, timpani, marimbas, bells, chimes, snare drums, tom-toms, music stands. There was nothing on the white walls — no pictures or posters, no diplomas or artwork, no distractions. We could sign up for only six hours a week in these rooms. Six hours a day wouldn't have been enough, so I sought out every empty hollow that squat little building had to offer. I took a tambourine up to the roof and practiced while watching a man run laps on the roof of the Chinese embassy across 66th Street. When the artificial light took over from the sun, I could see Broadway slice the crosstown streets, one blazing X after another. There were four floors of basement, so I took the elevator down with my snare drum and camped out in whatever cinder-block corridor happened to be deserted. Sometimes three or four of us would practice in the hallway in front of our studios, standing ten feet apart and trying to ignore each other.

Except for eight a.m., there were very few times when I got to school and stepped off the elevator on the third floor and didn't hear practicing going on. I would return from picking up some dinner, and by the time I came around the corner and passed the harp studio, I could hear xylophone or timpani or tambourine in the hallway. I knew it wasn't the same person practicing all the time, but it didn't matter — it was a reminder that someone was practicing and I wasn't. If I went for lunch or dinner, someone was still upstairs practicing. If I went to class, if I went to the bathroom, if I spent five minutes trying to clean up my locker, someone else was spending that time practicing.

A non-musician might ask: practice *what*? What, exactly, did "percussion" mean? When a regular person asked me what I played, sometimes I said, "Drums," sometimes "Percussion." If saying "drums" conjured an image of me behind a drum set performing with KISS, saying "percussion" elicited a stare as blank as a sheet of paper. Any accurate explanation of the instruments involved — drums, of course, but also xylophone, vibraphone, tambourine, triangle, and anything else you could shake or smack — was usually met with "Oh."

I heard a story from one of my new colleagues, Frank, a fellow percussionist, about an experience he had in the emergency room. One winter day, he skidded on an icy patch of sidewalk in front of his building and reached out to break his fall. What he grabbed was a railing with a serrated top ridge, a decorative row of pointed shapes designed to keep pigeons from perching there. It sliced his hand like a bread knife. When he got to the ER, he used his unmangled hand to whip out his Juilliard ID and lay it on the counter in front of the triage nurse. "I'm a Juilliard pianist," he told her, and he was promptly stitched up by the hospital's best hand surgeon. Frank, though in pain and shock, had thought quickly. "Juilliard" was easily understood; "pianist" was also immediately clear. In the time it would have taken to explain what percussion was, Frank would've bled out.

At Juilliard, I didn't have to explain percussion. My fellow students were narrowly focused, unathletic, apolitical, average-looking geeks. We may not have had the highest SAT scores, or even bothered to take the SATs — we may not all have known what "SAT" stood for — but every one of the students, even the dancers and actors, knew what percussion was.

If the odds were bad and the work hard, going to a music conservatory instead of a real college at least meant the decisions I had to make were limited. Nothing about classes or majors or even social situations. When to practice? *All the time. Now* and *later.* In high school, spending that much time alone was isolating and — at least for girls — isolation in high school felt like all the other baboons had moved on while you were sleeping and left you on the savanna to fend for yourself. I wasn't good at being in high school. I wasn't popular and, worse, I cared that I wasn't popular. I didn't know how to become popular like Suzanne Moore, forever immortalized in a year-book photo in which she showed off her savvy, her style: it is a close-up of her standing on the football field behind the school, squinting in the Saturday-afternoon sun and wearing an outfit — red jacket and black turtleneck — that matched the red background and black tongue on the Rolling Stones ticket she held next to her smiling face. *That* was being successful at high school, and no amount of practicing would make me better at it. Having Juilliard as a laser-focused goal was a gift; I wasn't happy, so I was living in the future where it was better.

Now my friends and I were toddlers at parallel play, alone together. Every morning I'd show up at seven thirty and sit in the lobby with Caroline. Since we'd met three years earlier at a national music camp, she'd been both my best friend and my competition. My first image on these mornings was of her hair: straight, black, parted in the middle, it would cover the sides of her face as she bent forward to focus on the lid of her coffee cup. Coffee ubiquity was decades away; we didn't yet have lids with the perfect opening for a mouth. These were the blue and white cups that decorated the desks in police procedurals. Caroline had to take the lid off in order to tear a perfect half circle on the edge. That accomplishment might cause her to shuffle her feet or maybe give a half smile, showing, at most, a few of her perfectly straight teeth. No more than that though — a full smile would've been aggressively cheerful considering the hour and the amount of work ahead of us. We'd spend a half hour on our bench, drinking coffee and orange juice and eating bagels while the lobby filled up with the rest of the early morning crowd. The only people allowed upstairs before eight were the blind piano tuners who would ply their trade during the only hours of silence a music school would afford them.

At exactly eight a.m. we crammed ourselves into the elevators, Caroline and I getting off at the third floor, the pianists continuing on to the fourth floor to hog their favorite pianos for the day. Caroline and I would stop at our lockers — giant closet-sized compartments that held our music, sticks, tambourines, triangles, snare drums — then head to whatever room or hallway or storage area we thought would give us a few hours of uninterrupted time.

As the days became shorter and colder, I became more neurotic. Everyone around me practiced furiously; everyone around me was driven to succeed. I began taking efficiency to a more obsessive level. After English, my only academic class, I would feel so desperate about having wasted the last hour and a half that I would run down the fifth-floor hallway, past the famous Ms. Dorothy DeLay's violin studio and the prodigies and parents who were always waiting to see her, past the glass doors of the library, and down the two flights of Stairway E to start practicing again.

Before the fall became winter, I would sometimes walk up Broadway to Vinnie's Pizza for dinner, then take my slice of grease and cheese and eat it on the way back to school. While I walked, I would practice rhythms in my head. This meant I had to keep steady time in my feet, which involved cutting a path through hundreds of people in the course of those 16 round-trip blocks, scouting ahead to find a path so I wouldn't have to slow down. Or I would get a sandwich at Sims Deli and eat it while walking around the fourth floor, looking for an empty practice room. I'd discovered I could practice in one of those rooms after dinner, when so many other drummers were looking for practice space on the third floor. The violinists and pianists didn't welcome me to the fourth floor. I never talked to any of them — I stepped over their outstretched legs as they sat in the hall, taking a smoking break — but they could not have appreciated that I was banging away in one of their rooms. The walls of these rooms were covered with heavy gold curtains, but that did little to muffle the sound of a snare drum or tambourine — or worse, cymbals, which to a pianist sounded more like construction noise than music.

}

One morning at the end of October, I took a practice pad and stool to the bottom of Stairway E. I'd discovered I could practice there even if someone was practicing above me on the third-floor landing. Nobody ever went down there; it was just an emergency exit. The only light came from an air shaft. The bottom of the shaft was covered with all the debris that had been pushed through the wire grating: tissues, plastic cups, pencils, gum, cigarette butts. I set up next to the exit door. The muffled noise of traffic droned in from Broadway. On the music stand, my metronome clicked.

I'd been practicing rolls and exercises for about two hours when a fly landed on the corner of my pad. I pushed my stick toward it, just touching it with the tip, and it flew away. Soon another appeared, and then more, lazily landing on the rubber part of the pad, flying away when I touched them, circling slowly above me, then landing again. I did this for a while, their buzzing low and constant in my ears, then decided to reach out and touch one with my hand. There was nothing there. I had been hallucinating.

I was thrilled. It was probably an indication of sleep deprivation — I was too anxious and excited to waste much time with my eyes closed — but I took the imaginary flies as a sign I was working hard.

At this point, I had no opportunity to prove in a performance that my effort was paying off. Playing a concert was ephemeral enough, the opposite of doing laundry, a chore I secretly loved with its piles of folded accomplishment stacked in front of me at the end of the task. But at least playing a concert was an end point, something to practice toward. I was placed in the lowest of the four school orchestras, the non-performing Conductor's Orchestra. It was as if we were part of a post-Depression make-work program, rehearsing pieces we were not ready to perform — Mahler's Fifth Symphony, Mussorgsky's *Pictures at an Exhibition* — slopping our way through them for six hours a week, only to then put them away and pick up something else. The conducting students of the school were the ones who led us through these majestic orchestral works, the blind leading the blind. Without a concert to gauge my progress, hallucinating flies was at least proof of my effort.

I hadn't been so focused even six months before. Just before graduating from high school I'd had my last physical with my pediatrician. Dr. Marx was nasty: his teeth, hair, and skin were stained yellow from the smoke of the cigarettes he never stopped sucking on, not even during my exam. He had an ashtray next to his typewriter so he could park his cigarette long enough to listen to my lungs.

Even though he was nearing retirement, it bothered him that his patients had already started to request his younger partner. In an effort to stay current, he decided he would ask about my mental health.

"What do you like to do? What are your hobbies?" Dr. Marx asked, blowing smoke.

"Well, I practice a lot," I said. Then I elaborated: youth orchestra, lessons, comprehensive music theory exam, piano.

Did I belong to any clubs at school?

Yes, I did. Band, jazz band, and orchestra.

He leapt on this. "Do you ever get so involved in music that you lose track of time? Do you ever stop playing your instrument only to 'wake up' and wonder where you are?"

"No."

"Do you have a boyfriend?"

"Yes."

"What are his interests?"

Having sex and smoking pot.

"Skiing," I said.

This seemed to reassure him. At least my boyfriend was not a musician. Exam over.

I was mortified. Never once had I lost time while practicing. I always knew where I was. My boyfriend was one of the amusical masses. This phlegm producer, Dr. Marx, had just pointed out my biggest shortcoming: I was unfocused.

Now, at Juilliard, the knuckles on my left hand sported permanently tattooed bruises from where the cymbal rested; I practiced so much tambourine, I scraped the skin off my right-hand knuckles and got blood on the head. I had *hallucinated flies*.

I had nothing to apologize for.

2

In the beginning . . .

Every Sunday of my childhood, I was dragged to church. One week when I was in seventh grade, our congregation had a picnic. Membership was declining, and they were attempting to make religion more casual and recreational. After the service, we ate a potluck lunch and then our pastor divided us into groups. We were going to have discussions.

In my group was a man named Mr. White. His daughter was in my Sunday-school class. He sat across from me at the picnic table, squinting in the sunlight.

"I have a question," he said, kicking off the discussion. "How could it be that Jesus was both man and God? Is He a man or a God?" Mr. White slammed his hand on the table. "I have a harder time with that than with the virgin birth!"

The adults at my table began throwing out their thoughts on Jesus: man or God. I wondered if Mr. White was so dramatic about everything. I imagined him at home, holding a tomato aloft and asking his wife, *Is it a vegetable or a fruit? I just don't know!*

Mr. White's passion for the subject made me aware of my own lack. In all those years, nothing about church had led me to experience a single spiritual feeling. Not the rote memorization, not the stained-glass windows, not the praying, not the Sunday-school lessons. Not even my fantasy that the pointy wooden cross hanging above the pastor's head would fall and slice him in half.

It's not that I would've been able to say what was missing. I only knew that I hated going to church, and every Sunday my sisters and I would complain that we didn't want to go, and our parents said we had to go, and we'd sit in the pew and sulk, and our parents would sit in the pew and beg God for better children.

The only reason I was allowed to miss church was youth orchestra. Most Sundays we rehearsed in the afternoon, but once a month or so we met in the morning. The opportunity to miss church was reason enough to love youth orchestra, but rehearsing gave me another: I found what I was missing in church. During my first year, we played Shostakovich's Fifth Symphony, and at the end of the piece everyone in the orchestra was at full volume: percussion pounding; strings sawing with long bows; trumpets soaring over the top while low brass anchored the bottom; the wind section screaming out high notes, trying to be heard. I don't know if the sound of an orchestra was "God" or "religion," because I really couldn't say what either of those was. But if "spirituality" involved a tightening of the chest that felt like grief, then spirituality is what I found.

♩

I loved music before percussion came along. I didn't play favorites: I liked it if I felt it. Some songs on the radio made me happy; some made me sad. Music was the simplest way to feel *something*. At that point, I didn't think about playing an instrument; I had no feeling that I might want to make music myself. I just loved to listen.

But anxiety about music was a companion, even then. The teacher of my third-grade general music class, Mr. Vaglio, liked me because I was enthusiastic about the subject, and I was thrilled and terrified that I would disappoint him.

One day he announced that the following week we would play "musical alphabet." My fellow eight-year-olds and I would stand in a circle and each of us had to say anything at all music-related that went with our letter of the alphabet. If you couldn't come up with "accordion" or "banjo" or "cello" when your turn came, you sat down — and eventually there'd be one winner left standing. If we had started playing that day, I might have been fine, but nothing ramped up my anxiety like time to think about my anxiety. I woke up the next Monday morning and told my mom I was sick. And the following Monday. And the one after that. By the fourth week I was confident about going back to school, certain the musical alphabet would have played itself out during that time. A winner would have been crowned, and I would not be exposed as the musical fraud I certainly was. I don't know if Mr. Vaglio was cruel or kind, but without ever mentioning why, he had put off the game for three weeks. When my turn came and the letter G settled on me, my frozen mind went blank. Mr. Vaglio counted down, giving me extra time, and then finally proclaimed me "out." Face flushed, I sat back down as

G moved on and Anna Parrish said, "Go-go dancing?" She beat me with *go-go dancing*.

With that kind of anxiety tailing me before I even began to pursue music as a profession, why start? Why not just play music as a hobby?

I started because, at that point, music didn't cause me any more anxiety than simply waking up in the morning and being a person. I was *always* anxious. My pink bedroom was my little fiefdom of utter control — every book, kitty statue, article of clothing, my throw rug, the few dolls I owned (and hated because they scared me) were all lined up at right angles. And I had a habit that would make an OCD specialist quiver with delight: I folded my garbage before placing it in the basket.

Anxiety was just a silent partner in those years, too integrated to stand out. The benefits of playing music were worth it. Learning this other language was like putting together a puzzle. I wanted to be special, to stand out, to do something few others could do. I'd always wanted to show off. When I was four, showing off took this form: it's summer and I'm playing on the sidewalk at our apartment complex with my friends. A group of men are walking back from the tennis courts. I remember their tennis whites and their rackets; I remember them laughing. I walk up to their group, face them, and yank down my pants. My friends are aghast. They freeze, horrified, with the exception of the one who runs to my mom and screams, "Patti pulled her pants down in front of *men*!" As I got older, the concerts I was playing in elementary school were a better way to show off.

In middle school, then high school, more and more of my free time was filled with music. I had percussion ensemble and youth orchestra; I played on recitals and entered concerto competitions. After school I went to Eastman School of Music's precollege program and took music theory and history and group piano lessons. (All non-pianists had to learn basic piano, yet none of us could really say why.) The summers after ninth and tenth grade, I went to Interlochen, a music camp in northern Michigan. Two summers at Interlochen cost the same as my parents' Ford Maverick. In my last year of high school, when my peers were taking SATs and writing essays, I was taking auditions. The schools sent out their catalogs with lists of required pieces for each instrument, and after months of practicing, I played for the college teacher at Eastman, drove to Cleveland and auditioned for their Institute of Music, and flew to New York and auditioned at Juilliard.

Good news was still delivered by mail in those days. Getting that fat acceptance letter from Juilliard was a crowning achievement. Now I would be the least talented, least qualified fish in a more exclusive pool — a pool that would not stop shrinking until we were competing at auditions.

3
The Peculiar Institution

At Juilliard in the 1980s, there was a long list of amenities the school did not offer: dorms, adequate practice space, rigorous academics, sports, fraternities, sororities, internships, exchange programs, attractive facilities, good ventilation, counseling, coddling, or hand-holding.

What we got instead were our teachers. For the 850 of us who filled the building in that autumn of 1983, the teachers were the reason we went to Juilliard. Lessons were one hour a week — just you, your teacher, and what you had prepared, alone in a room. If you were unprepared or even underprepared, it was a very trying hour. But if your habit was to try to slide by in a lesson, you were sorely lacking in understanding about music school. There was no hedging of bets at a conservatory, no violin with a side of accounting. No one entering a music conservatory was confused enough to think there would be a safety net: it was all or nothing. All — win an audition for an orchestra, get tenure and health insurance, and play music for the rest of your life. Or nothing — work for minimum wage selling albums at Tower Records until you could convince your parents to send you to a real school.

Physically, Juilliard was a strange place. The rooms in which we spent the most time — practice rooms, teaching studios, the listening library — had no windows. I was convinced, too, that there was no ventilation. I examined the thermostat in one of the studios one day, thinking I could turn up the heat, and found that beneath the realistic-looking cover were just a bunch of wires and a wadded tissue. So that was what the school had to offer: rarified air. We literally breathed the exhalations of our famous teachers.

Even though my principal teacher, Neil, was young and I'd already known him for three years — he'd taught at Interlochen during the summers — I was nervous in my lessons and desperate to please him. His focus for me, those first months, was to get me to "play out" — to play bigger and louder and more expressively so that I was playing for an audience instead of for myself. Every week, through September, October, and November, I'd set myself up across the studio from him, standing behind my snare drum. He'd tell me to play a loud roll. I'd give him the loudest, crassest roll I could come up with — arms laboring, mouth clenched, body rigid — I'd go for volume over quality, and come up with a sound like a jackhammer. He'd shake his head, tell me that his grandmother could play louder, and start writing out exercises for expanding my dynamic range.

Neil was as much drill instructor as teacher — ordered, utterly methodical, full of structure. He not only taught my lessons, he looked at the macro side of learning to play percussion, thinking about all I would need to learn. From what I knew about other schools — Cleveland

Institute, Temple, Curtis — this was how most percussion teachers taught. There was a set of skills to be learned on each instrument, and exercises and étude books to go through. There were standard pieces to learn, and the teacher would not only teach you the piece, he would tell you which pieces to play.

The timpani teacher, Donald, had a similar approach. Timpani — big copper drums that looked like fudge-mixing bowls — were part of percussion. A percussionist had to be at least an adequate timpani player, but at this level, most of us already had a preference — we wanted to play either timpani *or* percussion. Playing timpani involved all of the things I was bad at — identifying pitches, playing loudly. I was never going to take an audition to become the timpanist of an orchestra.

Richard, another percussion teacher, had an entirely different approach. He didn't tell us what to bring to lessons, what to work on or in what order. He sat on his stool, with a pair of sticks and a smile, and waited to see what you wanted to learn. Though Neil was my main teacher, I took extra lessons with Richard, something that was encouraged in a specialty that involved so many different instruments and techniques. Once I was in the studio with him, his teaching was magical. But it was up to me to know what I needed him to teach me.

In this way, Richard wasn't unlike Juilliard itself. If you came to the school with the drive to learn, all the tools you needed to succeed were available. While we were only in lessons one hour a week, we were, each one of us, alone many hours a day. No one stood over us in a practice room. By not supplying any guidance, it seemed like Juilliard was doing everything wrong. What they actually accomplished was weeding out the musicians who weren't smart enough or driven enough to figure out this process for themselves. In that way, it seemed exactly right.

❧

In the summer of 1969, a time when a very different kind of music-making was going on upstate at Woodstock, Juilliard had moved to its current location on the Upper West Side of Manhattan. What began as the Institute of Musical Art in 1905, and the Juilliard Graduate School in 1924, eventually combined to become the Juilliard School of Music in 1946. To reflect the fact that the school also trained dancers and actors, the name now spelled out in gold on the side of the building was simply *The Juilliard School*.

Inside the dim lobby, a fixture as permanent as the building itself sat at the guards' desk. Ireland had sent Nora over years before and now she greeted actors and dancers and musicians with a "Hellooooooo," and "Jesus, Mary, and Joseph," and, if you were lucky, the offer of a Lorna Doone cookie. Since Robin Williams would have passed her every morning during his time as a student, it was probably no coincidence that Mrs. Doubtfire looked just like her.

Odd creatures also filled the classrooms and the studios. Teachers weren't hired for their ability to conform. Juilliard was a trade school — not unlike an Apex Tech that trained refrigerator repairmen — and instructors needed only to excel at their craft.

My music theory class was taught by a composer who was married to comedian Chevy Chase's mother. With a wrinkled suit and wrinkled face, he'd walk into the classroom and fill the blackboard with problems to solve and then mysteriously disappear three or four times a class while we solved them. The English teacher, Mrs. Nelson, had a forehead creased like a shar-pei from her efforts to get generations of musicians to actually come to class and to care. She would drone on and on, filling her lectures with "Do you see?" and "Do you know?" when there was something she wanted us to see or know.

When I first moved to New York, I'd been lucky to find an apartment in the same building my friend Caroline lived in, the Beacon Hotel. While I waited for the previous tenants to vacate, they put me up in a temporary unit furnished with a bed, couches, towels, and fleas. So after taking Benadryl to suppress the itching these red patches caused me, I'd fall asleep when I had the time — that meant English class. Then I'd suddenly come to with a snort and wipe the crust from my mouth. There were only about a dozen kids in the class, far too few for me to go unnoticed as I drooled. Mrs. Nelson finally asked me to stay after class one day and I explained about the fleas and the Benadryl, and I think she was relieved that there was a reason I was ignoring her.

Closer to home, in an office between the two percussion studios, was our hunchbacked orchestra librarian. Whether it was because he was forced to listen to banging all day or due to his hump, Jackson was irritable. If the studios were full and the stairways occupied, we thought nothing of torturing him with a xylophone right outside his open door.

≀

After so many months spent practicing without performing, I was ready to polish a piece of music, put it on the
stage, and call it my best effort. There was a xylophone
solo I wanted to play, so I asked — begged, really — for
the chance to play it on our upcoming percussion ensemble concert. "Frivolity" was five minutes of running my
arms up and down the xylophone as fast as I could and
hitting little wooden bars that were only an inch and a
half wide. It was a high-wire act that demanded to be exe-
cuted perfectly: the melody was so tonal and recognizable
that any wrong note would linger like a fart in church.

Global anxiety had been a part of my life for as long
as I'd had a life, but that spring, as the percussion ensemble concert drew near, I finally found something to feel
nervous *about*.

4
Stage Fright, Part I:
The Seeds

Playing percussion had never made me nervous. I wasn't cocky; getting nervous just didn't occur to me. I had played concertos in high school — standing onstage in front of the orchestra wearing a pink Gunne Sax prom dress, looking out over the audience and feeling no different than I did when I played through the piece in my bedroom. Just one time, moments before starting my senior recital at Eastman, I had the smallest possible feeling that what I was about to do was a bigger deal than I'd given it credit for. This feeling took the form of wanting my teacher to stay backstage with me instead of joining the audience. As soon as I started playing, though, I forgot about that feeling.

Playing music had always been unconscious execution, like walking. Now, in the weeks before the percussion concert, I'd started to get this feeling of *awareness*. I'd be practicing "Frivolity" in the hall and suddenly I was aware of my hands moving, aware of my heart beating. Someone would walk by, hear my unintentional performance, and I would become aware that I was being scrutinized.

}

New York City had the same climate I'd grown up with upstate, and I knew that January, February, and March were indoor months — months for grinding work. There were no holidays to break the routine: it was dark and cold, and you stayed inside and practiced. In the early mornings, I woke up in my room at the Beacon and snuck into the bathroom. Across 75th Street, there was a parking garage; it was open 24 hours, always lit, and its blue glow shone into our apartment. The garage had low concrete barriers where its outside walls should have been, but there was nothing to watch, just cars circling from one floor to the next. Lana, a dancer, slept on the floor near me, but she went to bed late and woke up late; she never stirred as I crept around the room getting dressed. Technically we had a one-bedroom, but only if you could afford to live in one room and sleep in the other. Candace had long ago taken over the "living room" as a place to sleep with her boyfriend Hank, a bassoonist. Hank confused me; he was 26 and already married and divorced. He seemed to have lived too much to still be only in school.

During these winter months, the snow piled up in the gutter outside the revolving door of the hotel. I walked by the Beacon Theater every morning. Some days the garbage from the previous night's concert littered the sidewalk. Sometimes what remained were the concertgoers them-selves. At 73rd Street, I passed the first of the triangle-shaped parks created by Broadway — the only rebel among Manhattan's grid of streets and avenues — which cuts diagonally through the Upper West Side. I passed the 72nd Street subway station, which sat on its own triangular island, then passed in front of McDonald's and the final triangular park. For three blocks, Broadway and Amsterdam were busy crossing paths with each other; by 70th Street they had worked it out and the rest of my walk down Broadway was a straight line.

I passed the Broadway Bazaar, a store full of plastic things for the home, mostly containers to put other things in. In the next block was a piano bar. A sign out front read "Houston's on Broadway!" over a headshot of a smiling, curly haired man. I felt mortified for him. I passed the Jamaica Savings Bank and then a movie theater with only two screens.

That was the west side of Broadway. Separating the uptown and downtown traffic was a divide with park benches and trees. On the other side of the divide, I passed Gray's Papaya and the Bagel Nosh. At the beginning of the next block was a Love's Drugstore barker who handed out flyers for a "big sale," and at the end of the block stood a garbage can filled with the flyers. The Ansonia Station post office came next, taking up the whole block. Earlier in the year I'd been waiting in line to buy stamps and realized I was standing next to Betsy Palmer, the actress who'd had her head cut off in *Friday the 13th*.

Just before Juilliard was John's Coffee Shop on the east side and Tower Records on the west. We all spent time at Tower, pawing through the classical albums in the basement. Then, halfway down the block on 66th Street, was the entrance to school. Those three months before the percussion ensemble concert, "Frivolity" was what I was thinking about as I walked through the doors.

I needed advice. Two weeks before the concert I was at my post in the hall, waiting for Richard to pass by. I knew when he'd be at school to teach, and though my back was to the hall, eventually I heard him pass, the heavy shuffle unmistakably his.

At 63, Richard had been teaching at Juilliard for many years. He had been a student himself at Juilliard back when the building was up on 122nd Street. A big man, half as wide as he was tall, Richard was always tucked neatly into his clothes. He had the appearance of being barely contained: waist cinched by his belt, neck circled by his bolo tie, wrist kept in check by his watch, finger stuffed into his wedding ring. He wore a sweet cologne; if he hugged you, his smell would stay on your shirt. His head was big and bald with only a sweatband's worth of white hair circling from one ear to the other. And he was pale — when he sat on his stool with the white studio wall behind him, it looked like his forehead had no end, but rose up from above his glasses and blended into the wall. Richard was kind, always smiling, and happily gave his students his time and knowledge.

Richard usually arrived about a half hour before the beginning of his first lesson. He settled onto the bench outside the orchestra library to eat his lunch. He swung his feet back and forth as he got it out, just barely scuffing the bottoms of his shoes along the floor. Forward and back, forward and back, like a kid. His trench coat was neatly folded on the bench beside him, hat resting on top, black bag on the floor. He smiled when he saw me coming and moved his coat and hat to make room for me.

I stood. My mallets were still in my hands. I propped my foot on the end of the bench and played them on my leg. Seeing that I had a question, he raised his chin to me.

"So . . . what are you eating?" I demanded.

He turned the sandwich around so I could see. Eyes twinkling, he offered it to me and I took a bite.

It was sweet: a slab of cheddar cheese, roasted red pepper, thick mayonnaise, white bread. Except for the red pepper, it was a kids' sandwich.

"Good," I said. I handed it back. Then my heart quickened. "So, Richard, do you have some suggestions about nerves?"

Richard's face became serious. "Sure," he said. "First, you want to be sure to move slowly. Move to the instrument slowly. Pick up your sticks slowly. Put them down on the instrument slowly." Resting his sandwich on the Baggie at his side, he pretended to pick up sticks and delicately place them on the head of a drum. "Just nice and easy," he said. He picked up his sandwich and took another bite. "Of course, if that doesn't work, there are always pills."

He meant beta-blockers, brand name Inderal. Take enough Inderal before any situation that threatens your well-being — being locked in a tiger cage, playing a solo from memory — and your heart will refuse to pound, your hands refuse to shake. The first I'd ever heard that such a pill existed was at Eastman. I was talking to my pianist friend Noreen, who was older and already in college there. She knew of another pianist who took Inderal before every concert. Noreen couldn't believe it. "I don't think there'd be any point in being a musician if you had to do that," she said. I felt the same way. What would be the point?

I had heard Richard took Inderal, but it didn't seem unusual for him. Old men took lots of pills. For the rest of us it seemed like cheating.

"I don't want to do that," I said.

Richard shrugged happily, not offended, and went back to swinging his feet.

⁂

Before we played a single note, percussion ensemble concerts were ripe with the potential for disaster. Even as we waited offstage to begin, so much was possible because most of our instruments were already onstage. Rows of gongs secured with rope and duct tape hung from wardrobe racks we'd stolen from the drama department. Triangles dangled on fishing wire, cymbals were stacked on tables. Drums teetered on stands, waiting to fall over in their top-heaviness. Black towels were draped across the tops of flattened music stands; on them we laid rows of sticks. Each of these sticks had the potential to cause a chain reaction among its peers, dropping one by one onto the hard, resonating wood of the stage, or falling en masse, a big clatter like wooden wind chimes in a hurricane.

None of these cataclysmic events seemed to occur singly. Even a stationary instrument like a xylophone could add to the trainwreck if a triangle landed on it. Heavy pieces of metal never just fell — triangles bounced, cymbals circled round and round. Sticks rolled until they fell off the stage.

Then into this setup came the drummers. We would have to make our way around the stage, change equipment between pieces, maneuver in and around instruments.

One drummer alone might have to play three Chinese tom-toms and five paint cans, turn to one side and play a log drum, pick up a rattle with one hand, then reach over the drums and cans to turn the page with the other. The cord that supplied electricity to the vibraphone snaked across the stage, just waiting to trip a drummer who was too distracted to pick up her feet. The audience got more visuals with percussion than with any other ensemble. They could become nervous and maybe a little hopeful that something would go wrong.

I think the awareness I'd been experiencing was the realization that the potential for disaster existed not just onstage but also within me.

‰

At the concert, while the audience was applauding for the piece before my solo, I slowly picked up my sticks and moved toward the xylophone. I was aware that as soon as the audience stopped clapping, after they coughed, recrossed their legs, and consulted their programs, they would turn their attention to me. The hall would become silent. That expectant moment, into which all my recent *awareness* could intrude, needed to be as short as possible. So as soon as I stepped up to the xylophone, I slowly turned my head to make sure the marimba accompanists were ready. I felt a heightened sensitivity, a heightened awareness of the stakes. My hands were slightly shaky as I thought about teachers and colleagues in the audience and onstage, people who would know exactly how I was supposed to sound.

I took a breath and started into "Frivolity."

Afterward we celebrated at our bar, the Donegal. It had gone well in spite of my new fears, and the resulting relief was greater than if I hadn't been nervous at all. I would label my level of drunkenness that night as shit-can-hammered. *So that was nerves,* I thought. Later, this bout would seem so academic as to be laughable. But at the time, I was glad I'd experienced nerves and had a strategy for dealing with them. I'd conquered stage fright.

Or so I thought. This was the last performance during which my nerve problem wasn't yet explosive.

5
Competition and the Tribe

Growing up with three sisters, I knew the basics of competition — how to size up a plate of cookies, how to scramble into the station wagon. But not until the summer after ninth grade, when I went off to Interlochen, did I learn about competing in music. This camp in the woods of Michigan was for dancers, musicians, artists, and actors and was the first place many of us learned what it would be like to compete on a national level. Suddenly it wasn't just about turning the plate so the largest cookie was in front of you or being the first to call the "way back," it was about playing better than everyone else. It was about "Challenges."

Interlochen strove to be different in every way, including its barbaric weekly competitions called Challenges. Founded as the National High School Orchestra Camps in the 1920s, Interlochen had only progressed to the 1950s by the time I showed up in the summer of 1980. There were rules for everything. You could get kicked out for smoking a cigarette or stepping foot off the grounds;

you could get in trouble for not wearing your uniform properly. There were "checkers" at the head of the cafeteria lines, employees whose job it was to see that you came to meals wearing not only your camp-issued blue shirt and knickers, but also your belt, your badge, and your color-coded socks. My division, high school girls, wore light blue socks — highly visible because our knickers stopped at our knees.

The camp frowned upon modern dance (they liked ballet) and menstruating (with two toilets per cabin and 16 girls who all seemed to get their periods at the same time, it clogged the plumbing), but most of all they frowned upon sex. They assumed, correctly, that sex was the likeliest diversion from practicing, and therefore social contact between the sexes was highly regulated. We had "coed" times when we were allowed to wear regular clothes and let the boys come into our division for a barbecue. We had dances occasionally. Then there was "Date Gate." Located at the entrance to the high school girls' division, it was just a place to go with your date where you could hide in the bushes and make out, all while being watched by a counselor of each gender. These counselors had the perverted job of watching kids make out and breaking things up if a couple went beyond kissing. Real sex happened far away from Date Gate: in practice rooms, empty classrooms, in the backstage areas of Kresge (the main auditorium), on the roof of Kresge, and, reputedly, under a canoe one night as it lay beached on the sand along the lake.

The effect of all those rules was to make it irresistible to try and break them. A friend of mine from home sent me a joint in the mail; I had a near non-minor stroke after opening it while the cabin counselor was in the next room. Since there was no place to smoke it, my friend Zora and I locked ourselves in the bathroom and ate it off of a saltine cracker, then walked around the main camp, pretending to be higher than we actually were. Twice, I made out with another drummer in one of the few practice rooms that had no windows. I never went to date gate. Not only was it creepy, it also seemed like too much of a commitment. I was there to practice, improve, compete. Having a boyfriend would've felt like a distraction.

Some kids, like me, were at Interlochen on scholarship but many more were incredibly rich. Or their parents were. Like Andie Nichols, a girl in my cabin from Amarillo. She not only came to camp for eight weeks, but also went to the Arts Academy, the boarding school at Interlochen. Her parents were so rich they paid Interlochen to raise her. The camp frowned upon any display of wealth, so we wore uniforms. They wanted us to be judged on our ability and not our clothes.

And judge us they did. We arrived at camp and were given a placement audition and ranked in order of how well we played. The first six percussionists in the rankings were put in the best orchestra — the World Youth Symphony Orchestra. Whoever had come up with the name was out to tell the teenagers, *You are now playing on a stage bigger than your high school orchestra whence you came.* Everyone else had to play in High School Concert Orchestra. No matter where you started, every week there was a chance to rise in the rankings, or to fall, with Challenges.

Early in the week, our teachers chose an excerpt from the music we were playing in orchestra. We'd all spend the week practicing it. On Friday, we'd show up at the percussion studio, the six players from WYSO and the number one player from the concert orchestra. Five of us sat on wooden school chairs while the first two players stood behind us to play. The number one player from the concert orchestra would "challenge" the number six player from WYSO, playing the excerpt we'd been practicing all week. Then the number six player would play the same excerpt. The five of us, our backs to the players, would raise our hands to vote on who we thought played better. The teacher announced the results. The winner would then challenge the number five player. Instant dog-eat-dog. At the end, the principal player for that week would take the results to the office, where they would be printed and posted for everyone in the orchestra to see.

It was the first time I realized my sense of personal worth could be quite so tied up in how I did on the battle-field. It wasn't subtle — numbers don't give you a chance to pretend that you aren't being ranked. You walked around camp all week aware that you were *number three* or *number six* and — unless you happened to be number one that week — aware that some of your fellow musicians were currently *better* than you. Based on the initial placement auditions, I started out that summer in the fifth of six chairs in WYSO. At the end of the first week's Challenges, I had slipped down two chairs. This was not just a fall in the rankings; I would now spend the second week as number one in the *lower orchestra*. I was crushed. My teacher, Neil, who would later be my teacher at Juilliard, came looking for me after Challenges. It was an early kindness from him; he was just checking in, making sure I wasn't leaping from the rafters of the outdoor auditorium. After I cried in one of those win-dowless practice rooms, after I pouted and felt sorry for myself, I realized that there was an equation here and it was simple: work harder, practice more, and rise in the rankings. Even though our positions changed many times throughout the summer, week two was the only time I spent in Concert Orchestra. The following week I challenged my way back into the higher orchestra, and for the eighth and final week, I'd challenged my way to the first chair.

At the end of the summer, all the campers gathered in Kresge Auditorium for the announcement of prizes. There were merit scholarships for every age and every division, from juniors through high school and from dance to acting to music. When it came time for the awards for my division, I sat up in my chair, nervous and excited. We were seated by cabin and at the end of my row was our counselor, Judy. Earlier in the week, I had gone into our cabin and she and another counselor were sitting on her bed, talking. They stopped when I came in. The three of us just looked at each other until Judy said she was telling the counselor she'd heard I was being considered for the orchestra award. Then she let out a squeal and said she shouldn't have told me.

No, really, she shouldn't have. Sitting there in the audience, I imagined the sound of my name being called, preparing to get up from my chair and turn sideways, apologizing as I squeezed past the legs in my row. I was getting ready to wait through the announcement of the runners-up when they called my name.

Fourth runner-up.

I stood, cheeks flaming, while the other campers applauded. When the winner was announced, it was Caroline. I watched as she trotted down the aisle, then climbed the stairs to the stage. I sat in the back, aspiring.

Caroline was the enormous talent against which I measured myself as a musician and in her company I was always happy and anxious. She was self-assured, strong, and unbending. If she had fears or feelings of inadequacy, she kept them to herself. Caroline didn't gossip or talk about herself; she didn't complain unless it was for fun, and then she joined in, loudly. Her religion was hard work, reliability, and loyalty. If I asked her for a kidney, her only question would be "Right or left?" before showing up at my door with a cooler. Right from the beginning, Caroline was my gold standard.

§

At the end of my first year at Juilliard, I spent the summer in New Jersey. Like Interlochen, Waterloo was a summer festival — a place to remove even the pretense of classes and focus entirely on playing. We lived in the dorms on the Fairleigh Dickinson University campus and ate in the cafeteria. Playing for our supper meant there was a lot of real life we didn't have to waste time on: grocery shopping, washing dishes, paying bills. There were only four percussionists there, ample empty classrooms in which to practice and no rules about when to use them. Even my commute was short — I fell out of bed, walked across the dewy lawn, and was practicing by seven o'clock every morning. After six weeks of practicing, rehearsing, and concerts and a quick trip home to Rochester, I was on the bus back to New York from Newark International Airport. For 20 minutes we bumped along the New Jersey Turnpike, past the city of Newark and the stink of Secaucus, then exited onto Interstate 495. As the bus approached the last New Jersey exit of Weehawken,

Manhattan was straight ahead but invisible, hidden behind a rock wall. The bus made one last turn, a long, curving final approach to the Lincoln Tunnel, and suddenly Manhattan appeared. This was the postcard picture of the city: the narrow band of the Hudson, thousands of windows as dazzling as a tennis bracelet reflecting the sun. To the far right was the financial district, anchored by the twin Trade towers. Moving left, there was the big gap of the Village, the long section of low rises that made the island look like an unequal barbell. Midtown came next, then Columbus Circle. The Gulf and Western Building, just north of the statue of Columbus himself, rose high enough for me to pick it out from its neighbors. Starting at Columbus Circle and counting streets, I could find Juilliard. I was about to start my second year of school, and about to meet a new competitor.

Wearing gym shorts and tube socks, Sebastian arrived at Juilliard. He was 17 and looked 12. Puberty hadn't finished with him yet. He had a barely visible mustache, which was brown like his hair on one side but faded to blond on the other. From a distance, in the fluorescent lighting of the hall, it looked like he'd only been able to grow half. His hair was parted in the middle and feathered back. If it were an inch longer, he could've been TV heartthrob Keith Partridge.

Sebastian came carrying the stick bag he'd made from the leg of a pair of jeans, and my understanding about the existence of talent slowly and painfully changed. My self-sustaining truth had always been that "talent" — if it even existed — didn't much matter. I didn't see talent, I saw hard work; *that* was something I could control. If a concept wasn't coming easily to me, if I couldn't quickly grasp some technical aspect, I reminded myself that my advantage over more "natural" musicians was that I was willing to work harder. Dedication, drive, determination, discipline — I would pump myself up with those words and push myself harder than everyone around me.

At Interlochen and then at Juilliard, teachers, conductors, and other students had always talked about Caroline as being naturally gifted, which she was. But I saw her talent in music as just one possible outlet for her brilliance. Her mind made connections faster than other people's. She chose to dedicate herself to music, but she could've taken on any career and excelled.

Sebastian, however, was simply born to be a musician. He walked in the door with gifts already tucked under his arm: beautiful hands, a passionate love of music, a singer's understanding of breath and phrasing. He also had dedication and drive. He had the desire to take what he had and make it better.

With Caroline I could always salvage my ego by reminding myself that she was a year older than I. There was always the possibility that the distance I had to travel to equal her ability could be covered in a year. Sebastian had the nerve, the anxiety-producing audacity, to have skipped a grade as a kid. He wasn't just a year younger — he was *two* years younger.

I wanted to hide. My instinct was to run from him, put in earplugs, and curl up in a ball at the bottom of Stairway E. All high school girls know this trick: keep your inadequacies to yourself. Don't go to school with a zit on your forehead and don't ask Sebastian how he plays Bach with lines so smoothly connected that it sounds as if he's playing a wind instrument. That was one option. Then I would leave Juilliard with my tiny ego intact and the skills necessary to sell records at Tower. After they trained me.

So, fighting my instinct, I quickly talked myself into a game only I knew I would be playing. I was going to be strong by being vulnerable, smart by being dumb. I would ask Sebastian questions. I would show him how little I knew so he could show me how much he knew — keep my friends close and my competition closer. I was consolidating my tribe: Caroline was already my best friend; Sebastian I would have to reel in even closer.

6
Stage Fright, Part II:
Full-Blown Flower

Facing none of the novelty and all of the hard work, I started my second year. Neil had decided to stop teaching and Richard became my official teacher. I was finished with English and moved on to my second academic class: the History of Western Culture. Let the real schools examine Late Medieval Devotional Images of Iberia for an entire semester. We were going to learn the history of everything that had ever happened in the Western world. Even an overview of all the exciting parts, though, was not enough to hold our attention. We skipped, slept, drooled. At the end of the first month of class, Ms. Meyerson gave us a multiple-choice quiz. It had 13 questions, four possible answers for each. I scored seven percent, significantly worse than chance. *Spectacularly* worse than chance. If I had spent time studying, I would have been mortified.

But I had other concerns. After bumbling along in Conductor's Orchestra for a year, I was now assigned to one of the orchestras that would actually play concerts.

First rehearsals for these concerts were more intimidating than the performances themselves because we were performing for our colleagues, our most discerning critics. No one — certainly not audience members — knew better than those sitting next to us exactly how the part was supposed to be played.

To combat the stress, I prepared for my *first* first rehearsal as thoroughly as a doctor preparing for conjoined-twin separation surgery. My checklist for the triangle part I would soon be playing:

- Try out different triangles and beaters.
- Make my own copy of the part so I can mark it up in red pencil.
- Practice rolls.
- Listen to the music in the library.

Check, check, check, anally checked.

Spending time in the music library was the most important of these self-commandments. Most instruments in the orchestra played more than we did. Strings, especially violins and cellos, played the most, nearly all the time. Commanding the melody, their part *was* the music. Percussion was more about adding to the music that was already going on — punctuating with a cymbal crash, emphasizing the violin melody by doubling it on xylophone. We listened to the pieces ahead of time so as not to get lost in the music. "Getting lost in the music" didn't mean surrendering oneself to the emotions the piece evoked. It meant that, within those measures of rest before you joined in with your part, you got so thoroughly confused that you didn't know *when* to play that part. It meant the conductor might look at you, expecting you to start playing, and see only a blank, terrified look on your face, and that he might then stop and humiliate you in front of your peers.

It's hard to imagine having trouble counting. But when nerves were involved, that was exactly what happened. Suppose there were 24 measures of rest, and on the beginning of the 25th, a crash. The measures of rest are arranged in three groups of eight, four beats to a bar. It starts off easy — you're deftly counting along, *1*-2-3-4, *2*-2-3-4, *3*-2-3-4. But suppose you get distracted and suddenly realize you have just started counting a tenth measure. *10*-2-3-4. *Panic.* Now you have to subtract those two extra measures in your head and recognize that you're really on the second measure of the second group. The problem is, the music hasn't stopped, and in the time it took you to figure that out, *another* measure has passed. By the time you've figured out that you're in the second measure of the second group, it's actually the third.

Brass players also played less than the strings did, but when it came to ratio of time spent sitting to time spent playing, nobody beat percussionists. We were the grand masters of sitting on our chairs, counting and sweating. Tom Petty was right: the waiting *was* the hardest part. Playing a xylophone solo was hard. Sitting on a chair imagining catastrophes and *then* playing a xylophone solo was harder.

Percussionists were the Special Ops of the orchestra. Count, play, and get back out. Bruckner's Seventh Symphony was striking in its sheer wait time. Its four movements held only one cymbal crash. The percussionist would sit there onstage trying to look professional — hands folded, legs crossed, no looking around — and finally stand up, pick up those two pieces of metal, and fling them at one another. And then sit back down again.

To combat the confusion and doubt, I'd plant myself in the library at a turntable with headphones and an album, listen to the music, and write in cues. If I wrote in my part that there's a bassoon solo at the beginning of the second group of measures and I heard the bassoon come in, I'd know I was in the right place. Unless, of course, the bassoon player got lost and came in wrong.

The year before, there had still been times I would sit in the library and listen to music for fun. I was discovering music I hadn't heard before; I closed my eyes and listened to Ravel's *Pavane for a Dead Princess* and imagined some romantic scenario to go along with the piece — the fountain at Lincoln Center with a solitary figure sitting on the edge, dead leaves swirling around her. Different images came to me now. Even as I was setting the record on the turntable, I would imagine the horn player getting ready to play the utterly exposed solo in the Ravel, and instead of leaves and fountains I'd imagine him trying not to puke from fear. Or I'd listen to Rimsky-Korsakov's *Scheherazade*, and instead of imagining 1,001 nights, I would see myself standing in front of a snare drum, four other percussionists next to me, all watching. They would know the solo I was about to play. They would have been silently critiquing my playing all week during rehearsals. I'd hear the clarinet scales and, as I sat there in the library surrounded by other students bent over their turntables, my heart would begin to pound. No matter that I was just listening, no matter that I was not in front of an audience, my heart was *pounding*.

A tiny incident happened that fall, one small thing I could see as a warning only in retrospect. This was not the cry of alarm sounded by Paul Revere — this was before that, the urgent message to get up and *get dressed*. It happened during an orchestra rehearsal. There was a bad page turn in my part — the music went right to the bottom of one page and continued at the top of the next. Since Caroline was standing next to me and not playing at that moment, I asked if she would turn the page for me. I was holding the triangle in my left hand and playing with my right, and when Caroline leaned over to turn the page, her face was level with my right hand. My hand shook. On the outside it was just a mild twitch. In my head it was a convulsion. *Why is my hand shaking? Does Caroline see it? Is she looking at my hand or the music? Caroline would never shake. Caroline is utterly reliable.*

All that in the time it took for Caroline to stand up, turn the page, and sit back down. It was just a tiny movement, but the seismic shift was about to arrive.

ᘔ

By early November, most of the northeast was dark by dinnertime. Not Manhattan. Broadway carried on like it was midday. I left school heading uptown, stick bag over one shoulder, cymbal bag over the other. I had my first "gig" — a rehearsal with the Westchester Symphony, one of the many part-time freelance orchestras in the area — and was going to meet my ride.

Light spilled onto the street from inside Tower Records as I passed. (The store was changing. When I had first arrived at school, there was only a small section of the store devoted to CDs, while albums took up most of the floor space. Now every time I went in, the CD bins had grown and the LPs were being pushed against the wall next to the cassettes.) I passed the movie theater and the bank, and across Broadway, on the corner of 68th Street, the light from the new Food Emporium was blazing. Unlike the Korean delis or Zabar's, this was a real grocery store. Full-sized carts. A long line of cashiers. Thousands of products in economy sizes. Stand in the middle of an aisle surrounded by cans, jars, and boxes, and it would be like a field trip to the suburbs. You could pretend you were anywhere, like Ohio or Kansas.

At 72nd Street, I looked for the dark blue car that would be my ride. There was one idling at the corner of West End and when I got closer I saw a horn in the backseat. I got in and we headed north on the West Side Highway, up and out of the city.

This was my first time meeting Donna. With every street lamp we passed, I learned more about what she looked like. Thin. Straight brown hair. Dark circles under her eyes.

"So this is your first time playing with Westchester?" she asked.

"Yes."

She snuck a look sideways at me. "You know the conductor is kind of . . . paralyzed, right?"

"No, I didn't." I laughed. We had all kinds of ways of describing conductors' faults.

"Actually," she said, "he really is paralyzed." She'd guessed he'd had some kind of stroke and could now only control one side of his body.

Oh.

Donna was an easy companion. As we left Manhattan, passed the Bronx, and entered the suburbs, she told me about her life. The schools she'd gone to. How she'd roamed Germany for a time, studying with various teachers, hitchhiking, and staying with families that housed and fed her in exchange for listening to her play. Now she freelanced and lived with her successful horn-player boyfriend who was a member of the Metropolitan Opera section.

44

"So every day I get to eat shit," she said.

I had been thinking that myself. The Westchester Symphony wasn't one of the better freelance orchestras. For me, still in school and supported by my parents, the playing experience was great and the pay good. For her, trying to make her half of the rent, the playing level was low and the pay terrible.

After about an hour we pulled into a high school parking lot. It was eerie — too dark and too quiet. I didn't understand why people thought suburbs were safer than cities. Horror films happened in the suburbs. No babysitter in a regular Manhattan apartment ever got a call asking if she had "checked the children." If she did, she would only have to lower her magazine to see from one room to the next.

Only 18 months ago I'd been a student in a different high school, 300 miles from here. Being on the grounds at night had signaled a special event. This place had a strange feel of expectation to it. Donna led me inside to the auditorium.

On the ride up I'd been trying to imagine how the conductor would get onstage and then onto the podium. A wheelchair? An assistant? Once I was there, I was busy setting up and I missed it. Suddenly Mitchell was just there on the podium, perched on a high stool with arm-rests. He looked both young and old, as if his features had been drawn from two different people. His coal-black hair and unlined olive skin belonged to a middle-aged guy; his one saggy eye and half a saggy mouth were an old man's. His face was doing two things at once: concentrating and relaxing, frowning and smiling. One arm hung limply from the shoulder, its hand an anchor in his lap. His other hand held a baton. His head was

45

bent down slightly, studying the score.

Steve, Tim, and Kevin, three older guys from Juilliard, were busy setting up with me. There was supposed to be another drummer, Joe, who was married and long out of school. He lived in New Jersey and, to make money, drove a bread truck.

By the time we started rehearsal, Joe had still not shown up. For an hour and a quarter we worked on the overture. Donna was right, Mitchell used only one side of his body. I gawked shamelessly.

Years later, I would come to look at this opportunity as more than a chance to earn extra money and gain experience. This was a division for me, a real break between approaching music as I had always approached it, and how I would need to approach it from now on.

At that moment, though, it was still just a rehearsal break. I wandered out into the hallway and took in the gray-green tiles that started on the floor and continued halfway up the walls. I was feeling almost giddy. I was in a high school without being in high school and it reminded me of what I had escaped. I took a drink from an old porcelain fountain and when I got back into the auditorium, there was a conference going on around the bass drum. Steve, Tim, and Kevin were talking about the next piece we had to rehearse, *Capriccio Espagnol*. Joe was supposed to play snare drum, but he still hadn't shown up. We couldn't leave the snare drum out — of all the percussion parts, it was the most important.

I begged them to let me play it. I had just been on the edge of their circle and not a part of their discussion but I made a case for myself. The part I was assigned to play was far less important and wouldn't be missed. Steve was principal for this concert, and it was really up to him to decide. Of course, one of the three of them should have done it — they were all older and more experienced. But I was the only one begging. They were the residents; I was the young med student asking to do the spinal tap.

Steve said I could play it.

After the break we started with the third movement. It was a short passage with thick orchestration and loud snare-drum playing. It was like singing in a chorus: surrounded by sound and contributing to the sound, but part of a group and therefore not exposed. I was playing on a crappy snare drum in a crappy high school auditorium. The orchestra sucked, and I wasn't exactly playing smooth rolls myself. But none of that mattered. It was fun.

The fourth movement begins with a loud snare-drum roll. It starts immediately after the chord at the end of the third movement has died down. Mitchell pointed to me and I played — a loud, glorious, imperfect, choppy roll. The brass section came in with their noisy fanfare and I continued playing, making crescendos and diminuendos with them. As the end of their fanfare approaches, the music gives no warning that the mood is about to change dramatically. The first-time listener has no idea that the brass is about to fade away, and the snare drummer will go from a loud roll to a very soft one. No reason to suspect that, of all the musicians onstage, soon, there will be only one playing — the snare drummer. I remembered, then, something Richard had said about this moment — when the brass finishes their cadenza and you're all alone playing a soft roll waiting for the violin to come in, it feels like you're standing there with your pants down.

The most astonishing part of what came next was that my body gave absolutely no warning. There are nerves

47

and there is panic and then there is all-out fear. It was only at the exact moment that I made my diminuendo down to the soft roll and was suddenly playing by myself that my body betrayed me.

Never have I been more surprised. A phrase came to my mind, one I used to laugh at, one that might explain what I looked like to those who were suddenly watching me: the conductor; my fellow percussionists; the brass players, who were just taking their instruments away from their lips; the woodwinds, who had to turn to their right; the string players, who, breaking all orchestral protocol, one by one turned completely around in their chairs to see why the snare-drum player wasn't playing:

I was shaking like a dog shitting peach pits.

My hands were no longer under my control. They shook so wildly, jerked so unpredictably, that I had to lift my sticks above the drumhead to keep them from making random swipes at it. I turned to Steve, who was standing closest to me, and helplessly held my sticks out to him. He held up his hands, confused, and stepped back.

On the podium, Mitchell appeared to be snarling. Half of his face was exhorting me to begin, the other half was indifferent. The effect was monstrous. With his good hand he gestured to me. "Play," he said, baring the teeth on one side of his mouth. *"Play."*

I lowered my shaking sticks to the head and moved my forearms stiffly up and down. Some semblance of a roll came out. It sounded like sneakers tumbling in a dryer.

The concertmaster started his cadenza and finally the strings turned around; the winds and brass faced their stands again. My ears were roaring. I continued to play but could hear only the white noise in my head and the sound of my heart, beating faster than it was meant to go.

48

It was only later that I could appreciate that my first time had happened in a rehearsal. I was grateful it hadn't happened in a performance, where the stakes would have been much higher. For the moment I was only stunned.

Donna said nothing about it on the way home. What was there to say?

The next day I was in a doctor's office. He interviewed me about my problem. No physical exam — he wasn't interested in my blood pressure or heart rate, and I didn't know enough to care that he should be. He gave me a prescription for 20-milligram tablets of Inderal and told me to take two an hour before a performance. With one disaster, I had immediately embraced the idea of taking drugs.

}

This was a sea change. Some people like surprises; control freaks do not. I could think of nothing I enjoyed less than the *unexpected*, especially when it involved potentially derailing the career I had chosen. Conquering nerves was supposed to be part of our struggle as musicians. Once a tightrope walker masters the technique of traversing a piece of rope, there is nothing monumentally difficult involved in inching along a foot off the ground. Learning to balance is one thing; walking between the World Trade Center towers is another. Inderal didn't make you faster, stronger, or better, but it offered the possibility that what you played for yourself in the practice room might be duplicated onstage when there was an audience watching. I now had a big secret, and I couldn't talk to Caroline or Sebastian about it. With 15 seconds of humiliation and a subsequent visit to the doctor's office, I had — for the time being — taken the entire question of nerves out of the equation.

But, as monumental as this shift was, I was too distracted to give it much thought. I had solved it — I had other things to worry about. Much of the practicing I would do that winter was preparation for the summer festival auditions in March. Waterloo — the one I'd gone to after my first year of school — was good playing experience but was not one of the most competitive to get into. For us, summer festivals were as important — maybe more important — than school. They were our internships. Many of the string and wind players went to festivals that concentrated on chamber music. The rest of us had our eyes on the big orchestral festivals.

I wanted to go to the Colorado Philharmonic. "Colorado Phil," we called it, like the festival was a one-eyed poker player. It was boot camp for orchestral musicians. Nine weeks, 27 concerts, 80 rehearsals — about one thousand students auditioned every year, and about 75 got in, including one timpanist and three percussionists. The festival's music director was short and everyone made fun of the way his arms got going in circles when he conducted, but no one doubted he could pick a great orchestra.

The audition for the festival was a short version of those I would eventually take to get a job — the process was the same. Get a list of excerpts in the mail. Listen to the excerpts. Practice the excerpts. Play the excerpts for other musicians and get their feedback. Obsess about the excerpts.

In the dark January mornings after Christmas, I'd get dressed for school, listening to 1010 WINS radio talk about Bernhard Goetz — how he'd been riding the subway when four kids asked him for money and, instead of ignoring them and staring off into space, he pulled out a gun and shot them. Then I'd go to school, practice all day, have my lessons with Richard, and, afterwards, I'd take my pencil and paper and sit on the bench in the hall. Ignoring the noise around me, I wrote down everything Richard had said before I forgot. *Accents are throws, not hits. Keep your jaw relaxed. Put out all the energy on the first note, and the second and third notes in that same hand come for free. Think of soft rolls in groups of fives or sevens so the measured pattern of lefts and rights isn't heard. Relax your shoulders down. Relax. Relax.*

I was focused. As hard as I was working, I wasn't tired; as tough as the odds were, I wasn't doubting myself. I wish I could've bottled this superpower — I was so focused I could've started a pile of music on fire just by staring at it. I had the perfect amount of pressure pushing me forward: I was aware that Caroline had gotten into Colorado Phil after her second year of school; I was aware that Sebastian was also auditioning this year. What I *wasn't* doing was catastrophizing — *What if I don't follow in Caroline's wake and it takes me until my third year to get in? What if Sebastian gets in but I don't?* No audition disaster scenarios ran through my head and I didn't spend any time contemplating a back up plan for the summer. I just practiced.

Then, at the end of the day, I'd go home and get undressed and listen to an update: Bernie Goetz had turned himself in, and New York was cheering his vigilante justice. Over the weeks, cooler heads prevailed and the news slowly changed — commentators talked about racism and innocent bystanders, regular New Yorkers admitted to wanting to shoot someone now and then.

My playing gradually morphed, too. Getting ready for this audition, some load of bricks finally fell on me about practicing — the quality mattered as much as the quantity. I had to concentrate on what I was not good at and try to fix the problem. I would be practicing away, my third hour of snare drum in the stairwell maybe, and suddenly I would *get* it. I'd play through Prokofiev's *Lieutenant Kijé*, and all of the little grace notes sounded like pearls, laid out in a line, all the same size and shape. Or I'd warm up on xylophone and then tape-record myself playing through the excerpts. I'd listen to the playback — the right notes in a steady rhythm, right tempos, right style — and it would occur to me that I could actually win an audition. It was no less thrilling than thinking I could win the lottery.

♪

I walked into my Colorado Phil audition. There was the conductor, veteran of thousands of auditions, waiting for me to play beautifully or badly or somewhere in between. Thanks to two orange pills I'd swallowed, I knew my hands were not going to shake, my heart was not going to jackhammer through my chest wall. I spent all my musical energy playing through my Bach sonata on marimba, then moved on to the excerpts, concentrating no longer on music but on achieving technical perfection, the pursuit of which could not have pleased my obsessive-compulsive disorder more. I walked out, smiling, knowing I had played the best I could have.

Within two weeks, I got my acceptance letter. And Sebastian got his. The third percussionist and the timpanist were also from Juilliard that year, so in June, the four of us would head to Colorado.

7
Real Pretend Job

The skills we used at an audition to get *into* an orchestra were not entirely the same skills we needed once we started the job. To get in we had to have "chops" — flat-out technical skills like the ability to play fast, cleanly, in tune, and in time. Those were the skills we chased during all those hours alone in the practice room. But if I were lucky enough to win an audition, I would need to get through a two-year trial period before I was given tenure in the orchestra. Learning how to play with other musicians *in* the orchestra was a different skill. That was where summer festivals came in.

Leaving the Denver airport, heading west and up, 75 of us arrived at the tiny town of Evergreen, over 7,000 feet above sea level. Most of us were in our early 20s, a couple were teenagers, and a couple of old ones were in their mid-20s. We were staying in two coed dorms that resembled ski lodges. Every day was hot and we were all still young enough to be courting the sun on our faces. In the afternoons it would rain just long enough to clear us off the patch of grass between the lodges we called the beach. At a mile and a half closer to the sun, my skin got darker and my hair got lighter; it took on the white-blonde color on a Miss Clairol box. We were surrounded by woods with shades of green we didn't see in the east, like sage and juniper, and columbines, the state flower. Except for the absence of a paycheck, this was like having a real job. We rehearsed in the morning, drove back to the lodges in the afternoon, squeezed in some individual practice time, then rehearsed again or played a concert at night.

When we practiced for auditions, our goal was to play the excerpts *in time*. Practicing by myself, I'd put on the metronome, the little mechanical tyrant that beat 60 or 80 or 105 times a minute, and I had no choice but to play along with it, neither speeding up nor slowing down, just marching along like a soldier. That was the goal through all those hours of practicing — to play as if the metronome was beating even when it wasn't. Then we got to rehearsal and had to forget everything we'd learned.

Conductors were their own metronomes. Our job was to follow. A conductor, even when he was trying to conduct in time, frequently wasn't. There might be a *ritard* or an *accelerando*, or he might just decide to stretch the tempo a bit or simply have no idea he was rushing or dragging. Even a good conductor might find himself pulled in different directions while playing traffic cop for so many musicians. Whether he was right or wrong, he was right. We had to follow.

The problem with "following" was that we had to look at the conductor. Not such a problem for trumpet or flute or almost any other instrument; those players' fingers gave them the feedback they needed so that they didn't have to look at what they were doing. The first time we rehearsed *Lieutenant Kijé*, I got myself set up and ready to play the snare-drum solo at the beginning. Since we knew the whole summer's repertoire before we got there, I had already practiced it endlessly. I had gotten passably good at having all the grace notes sound alike when I was staring down at the drumhead, but when I looked up to wait for the downbeat I lost the one direct connection — sight — that I had to the drum. There was a stick between my hands and the head. I had to learn to practice looking up and relying on muscle memory.

Mallet instruments posed an even greater challenge. No sensation comes through the mallet to let you know you're about to hit a wrong note. You only hear it afterward. From playing in rehearsals, I started to learn how to compensate — sneaking a quick glance during a rest or trying to position myself so I could peripherally see both the instrument and the conductor.

There was no way to learn these lessons at school. With the Juilliard orchestras, we might play four or five big concerts a year. Here we played three a week.

Sebastian and I rotated the principal percussion duties with Rick, a master's student who'd just finished his first year. For each concert, one of us would be in charge of breaking down the music into assignments for each player. If I was playing snare drum on *Lieutenant Kijé*, I might also have to play sleigh bells, or triangle, or cymbals later in the piece. The parts had to be divided so that each player had time to get from one instrument to the other. Then the principal would look at all the parts he'd just created and hog the best one for himself.

The rest of the musicians that summer came from the other big conservatories — Curtis, Cleveland Institute,

Eastman, Oberlin, Peabody — and a few even came from universities. My roommate, a bassoon player named Jennifer, had just won an audition for the Utah Symphony and would be starting as soon as the festival was over.

Jennifer was much further along in life than most of us there that summer; not only did she have a job, she had a fiancée. Jason was an Eastman graduate and a failed trumpet player who was spending the summer in Salt Lake City, setting up his new optical practice and waiting for Jennifer to join him. Musicians like Jason terrified me — he'd given up so quickly. Had I met Jason when he was just out of high school and heading off to Eastman, I would've pulled him aside and offered some advice: practice a lot harder. No, really — when your friends want to go out for pizza and beer and you're feeling so liberated and grown-up and just plain happy being away from your parents that you think, *I'll practice afterward*, and then afterward you're tired and buzzed and just decide to go to sleep, just tell your friends, "Next time," and keep practicing because all of those times add up. And if he was really serious about marrying Jennifer and didn't want her to find someone else, he should put off starting his new and boring career and spend the summer in Evergreen.

Because, in sum: youth, hormones, coed dorms, sun, fresh air, tans, free time, woods, beer, pot — Jason had no chance. By the end of the first month, Jennifer was disengaged from him, going out with my fellow drummer Rick, and the box of wedding invitations had been pushed under the bed.

≀

It was good I had been forced to ignore any qualms I had about taking Inderal. At school I played a concert once every six weeks; here I played one every other day. Any time I had a part that was remotely hard or exposed or soft or all three, I would hide myself in the girls' bathroom with my knapsack and stash, perfecting the art of slipping the drugs under my tongue and getting to the drinking fountain, or sometimes just cupping my hands and drinking at the sink. I took it for rehearsals and I took it for concerts.

I did have pangs of guilt now and then. When we performed Ravel's *Bolero*, Sebastian and I took turns playing the snare-drum part. It wasn't technically hard, but the beginning was utterly exposed — just snare drum and a few plucking strings, the quintessential eggshell snare-drum part. With chemical help, I only had to concentrate on playing the same two measures for 15 minutes. On the bus ride home after the first concert, Sebastian was quiet. When I asked what he was thinking, he said I had just played the most perfect *Bolero* he'd ever heard. I felt good and a little bad, but not bad enough to tell him I had cheated.

That Sebastian admitted to feeling vulnerable, even obliquely, was a rare moment for him. While I was spending the summer trying to recover my confidence after one traumatic rehearsal, Sebastian was displaying his fearlessness. He was a musician who appeared completely unafraid. I wanted to stand close enough to him to be covered by his shadow. It was time to further consolidate the tribe.

The morning after our Fourth of July concert, complete with fireworks, Sebastian and I were on the bus waiting to go to rehearsal. My friend Amy got on. She was a viola player from New England Conservatory. She'd been busy since arriving in Evergreen, sleeping with three different guys already — although economically, two of them at the same time. She saw me sitting with Sebastian and leaned over and whispered that I should go for it.

Already went.

Sebastian and I were isolated in the Colorado woods, playing together, eating together, even riding the bus together. We'd already been good friends at school, but a relationship that would've taken months to develop in New York was condensed into weeks. He was just barely older than when I first met him, 18 now, to my 20. At that age, two years mattered. I still saw him as very young. But nothing could've attracted me more than the way he played. There was no better aphrodisiac for me than smooth rolls and perfect grace notes. I saw him and heard him every day: the care he took with the parts he played in orchestra, his attention to detail, the way he crafted music out of the most technical of passages. I was in love.

Dennis — Sebastian's roommate — had paired up with a violinist, and now that Sebastian and I were a couple, the four of us spent our free time at Sebastian and Dennis's host parents' house, sitting in their hot tub and watching the moon progress across the sky. We talked about the festival: about the cook, who, because of her beard, we'd named Hairy and who had made me an instant vegetarian after I'd spent a night over the toilet, puking up her undercooked beef casserole. About the walk along a dirt road Sebastian and I had taken earlier in the summer, where we'd come upon a bull standing next to a fence and I'd tried to persuade Sebastian to· pet him so I could take a photo and how, instead, I'd ended up with a picture of Sebastian, arms crossed, looking warily at the bull. There was a coda to the story, which Sebastian brought up constantly, a newspaper article about a bull who'd escaped his confines and gored a nine-inch hole in the stomach of an onlooker. We were in a bubble there in Evergreen — a foxhole mentality developed from living with so few other people for nine weeks — and we talked about the other pairings that had occurred or were occurring that summer, avoiding mention of Dennis's fling in the dirt with a musician who admitted she took valium before difficult concerts, and steering clear of Amy's recent past once she started joining us in the hot tub and began to get to know the host couple's 15-year-old son.

Now that I had Sebastian's attention, I decided it was time for him to teach me to play cymbals as well as he did.

Bad cymbal playing audibly validated every stereotype other musicians held about drummers. A good cymbal crash could punctuate the climax of a Mahler symphony like thunder and lightning; the soft scraping together of two cymbals could evoke a sword being pulled from its scabbard. A bad cymbal crash was just bad. It was physically jarring, like reaching forward with your foot for an extra step and stomping on air. There was a curve in each cymbal from its outer edges to the small dome at the middle. If we hit them together too squarely, an air pocket would suck the energy out of the crash, making a sound like popping a paper bag.

Cymbals are exceptionally unforgiving: clapping your hands together when each holds a three-pound slab of brass takes courage. You couldn't start softly and sneak in or take it back once it was out there. And if I got distracted, a quick thought would run through my head — that a sin of omission was sometimes better than a sin of commission. If I left out a large cymbal crash, the conductor would notice. But if I came crashing in where no one was expecting it, the players directly in front of me might slide right off their chairs.

Sebastian stayed at the school with me after rehearsals and we practiced in the band room. I held a pair of 20-inch cymbals and Sebastian stood behind me, chin resting on my shoulder, arms wrapped around me. He covered my hands with his and, like this, we played crashes, until I began to understand what it was supposed to feel like to make the kinds of sounds he did.

Sebastian was also reminding me that I still loved music. The Westchester rehearsal had been such a painful discovery — I'd certainly never thought I was invincible, but how humbling to discover just how vincible I was. That had sucked a lot of the fun out of orchestra playing for a while. Sebastian listened for fun all the time. We would sit in his room and he'd play tapes for me on his Walkman. We'd talk about the tapestry of sound of the organ-grinder section in Stravinsky's *Petrushka*, literally like a wall hanging with so many colors and textures woven together that you know what you're hearing is the sound of a carnival; or the moment in Tchaikovsky's *1812 Overture* when the cascading eighth notes finally end and the snare drum gets to announce the last section with a loud *ruff*! I remembered to slow down and enjoy the moment near the end of Mahler's Fifth Symphony when two brass chords sound like the opening of the gates of heaven. Sebastian would play the end of Schumann's Second Symphony over and over so we could hear the glorious sound of the timpani solo, just two different notes. No matter how many times we listened, it was joyful, as uncomplicated as the joy of a dog lighting up when he sees his leash. We'd listen to Beethoven's Fifth Symphony — not the famous first movement but the cello melody of the second. Three times the cellos played it, slightly altered each time, with a brass fanfare between each repetition for the listeners to collect themselves. It was heartbreaking because it was beautiful and because it lasted only for those 24 measures and then it was gone.

By the time we headed back to the sweet stink of New York in August, I'd learned an approach to improving my cymbal playing, and learned, if not always *how* to follow a conductor, that I at least needed to practice doing so, and played 27 concerts and about 80 rehearsals. I was halfway through four years of school and ready to settle back into the trenches with Caroline and Sebastian.

8
Girl Drummer

Back when I'd been a newly minted ten-year-old drummer, I had a crush on Todd, the sixth grader playing snare
drum next to me. He was vastly older and more experienced than my fifth-grade self, and I admired his stylish
Davy Jones haircut, but I admired his percussion skills
even more. Todd, unfortunately, had no interest in me.
That was the extent of my first drummer crush.

Now, even though I was not yet employed, falling for
drummers carried more risk. Leaving a trail of breakups
with my future colleagues could have repercussions. But
what could hold a greater attraction for me than the same
skills I myself wanted to possess? My first year at school
I'd gone out with a drummer named Aaron. After he
graduated, he moved in with his parents to practice and
take auditions, leaving Juilliard and me behind. He was
so much further along in the process that we were not
really competitors. That was not the case with Sebastian.

By 1984, being a girl drummer both was and wasn't
a novelty. There were times when it didn't occur to me

— my teacher at Eastman precollege was a woman, and during my first year in youth orchestra the percussion section included four girls besides me. But as I grew older, the ranks thinned and the sections overwhelmingly became sausage parties.

Token appointments of women in professional orchestras in the 1930s — a harpist and a cellist in the Philadelphia Orchestra, a horn player in the Pittsburgh Symphony — became proportions nearing 40 percent by the mid-1980s. But there were still imbalances within instrument groups in orchestras: there were many more women harpists than low brass players, far more women flutists than percussionists.

Girls my age — not just in music — were still figuring out where we stood. The women of the '60s had paved the road so well that we barely noticed or thought to look back. We were told to go out and support ourselves. Be independent.

Truthfully, we didn't need to be told. All my '70s girlfriends and I knew the '70s moms who smoked cigarettes and downed valium and said, "Sure, go play with the chainsaw," and tried to dull their awareness of being stuck and frustrated and terrified of being dependent on a man. I was starting to see a new group, '80s moms now, jogging with their strollers in Central Park, trying to work off baby fat as a group, led by a militant coach who ran alongside them and yelled out moves like "Double hold!" and the mommies would face forward with both hands at the helm; "Side step!" and the mommies would place one hand on the stroller and skip sideways. These high-powered moms took all their creativity and energy and poured it into a corporate approach to motherhood. I was horrified by them.

Occasionally I ran into the opinion, baldly presented as fact, that women weren't as well suited as men to playing percussion. When I auditioned for the Cleveland Institute of Music as a percussionist (unlike most schools, Cleveland auditioned their incoming students as either percussionists or timpanists), I was still required to play a short timpani audition. After I finished my étude and solo, the timpani teacher walked over to me and stood on the other side of the lowest drum. He asked me to play a loud roll. I played one. "Louder," he said. I played louder, but before I was even finished he was making a face. Taking the sticks from my hands, he backed up and said, "I meant like *this*." And here, not unlike a caveman beating on his chest, he unleashed a series of blows that rained down on the poor drum like a golf ball hailstorm. Then he told me they didn't usually accept women as timpani students. When I asked why not, he said, "Because they usually aren't very good."

Not that I wanted to get a job playing timpani. By the time we got to school, most of us gravitated to either percussion or timpani. I had always liked percussion better or feared timpani more, or both. Some drummers — like Caroline and Sebastian — were great at both. And even though most auditions now were for either percussion or timpani jobs, I still could not ignore timpani. There was usually one player in each percussion section who doubled as assistant timpanist; not being able to play timpani would cut out that whole category of auditions for me. And there was something else. Not being able to play timpani made me feel like I was wimping out — I didn't want to be a *girl* who couldn't play timpani, because then I might be the girl who couldn't play timpani because she was a girl.

I had an incident at Interlochen one summer, the kind

of experience I would call a stress dream had it been only a dream. One morning, on the stage of Kresge, we were rehearsing Mahler's Fifth Symphony. The week before I had challenged my way up to first chair and got to pick the best part for this week's concert. Timpani.

On the podium was a conductor named Kenneth Andrews. At the time he loomed large in my mind. He was strict, always starting rehearsal precisely on time, never cracking a joke or even a smile. He yelled at the percussion section if we weren't following a score when we weren't playing. He was a petty tyrant and a bully, and I feared him.

There is a section in the first movement of the Mahler where the orchestra suddenly stops, the brass play two chords, and then the timpani comes in with a loud and glorious solo. It lasts only half a measure, but if the timpanist doesn't fill that space it's as if the bottom dropped out of the sound. So the orchestra stopped, the brass played their two chords, and — feebly — I played my timpani solo. Not majestically, not grandly, and certainly not loudly.

I was lost. I wasn't playing softly because I couldn't play louder, but because I wasn't confident about where I was in the music. That's not what the conductor thought. He stopped the orchestra. The sound ground to a halt, as one instrument and one section after another realized we'd stopped playing. Kenneth slammed his baton on his music stand, then pointed it at me. The whole orchestra turned and stared.

"Never play like that in my orchestra again!" he screamed.

How I played after that wouldn't matter to him. I could've used concrete mallets and ripped through the heads and it wouldn't have changed his mind.

The next day Kenneth yelled at the violins. He made them play a section on their own, and they played it timidly. "You play like Patti!" he screamed. My name had become synonymous with *timidity*. Later that day I ran into him in the orchestra library. I had checked out a score to the Mahler and was writing cues in my part. I held up the score to show him I wasn't going to get lost again and gave him a nervous laugh.

"That's not the problem," he said. He grabbed my upper arm. "You need to eat your Wheaties."

ʒ

During my first year at Juilliard, one of my schoolmates told me he didn't think there were any good women timpanists "out there." I didn't bother to explain to him his faulty reasoning — as there were no professional women timpanists "out there" then, he was performing an apples-to-oranges comparison of professional male timpanists to women timpanists who were currently students. The practice of "blind auditions" (playing behind a screen) that most orchestras implemented in the 1960s and '70s was certainly taking away the perception of bias; the actuality couldn't be far behind.

What would affect me more was being a girl in the midst of so many guys. We stood out to our colleagues and stood out to our teachers. That fact would be the cause of consequences far more serious than a few morons who wanted to bait me by telling me that only boys could be drummers.

9
Perfection

One night, during my third year of school, I went to hear a concert in Carnegie. Sitting close to the ceiling of the great hall, looking down at the tiny percussionists and their tiny instruments, I was there for Bartok's *Music for Strings, Percussion, and Celesta.* I wanted to hear the piece played live because the xylophone part was one of the excerpts we would be asked to play at auditions. When they got to that section, what came out was not what I'd heard many times on recordings, but something that Bartok had not written. As I would repeat to my colleagues in shock and glee: the percussionist stepped all over it. The glee was relief that even the best drummers made mistakes.

Rationally, it was obvious to a listener that it was unfair to compare a recording to a live performance. Even live recordings weren't all live: if the orchestra made a recording of this Carnegie performance they would have added a quick "patch" session at a later time to cover any mistakes and seamlessly plugged those perfect patches into the mix. Still, this promoted the illusion that mistakes didn't happen. Even, like this, on xylophone, where a mistake was so obvious. Oh, the glory and the terror that we had to master an instrument that could be so perfect. Not like a violin or a flute: their notes could be sharp or flat, or short or long. For us there was only one pitch, right or wrong, rendered in one short length on an unforgivingly resonant piece of wood.

In high school, the goal was to practice and rehearse, then enjoy the performance. Now I was beginning to feel that there was no way to make it a win. I started at zero. If I played perfectly, it was still zero. The best I could expect was to *not fail*.

In the ten months of concerts I'd played since my disaster in Westchester, I'd been fearless. Dulled by Inderal, certainly. It was just that my anxiety meter ran so high, the Inderal did not dull my concentration or make me want to nap. The effect was to pull me off the ceiling and prop me onstage with a heightened yet tolerable awareness of the performance I was about to play. It made me fearless. I knew my hands would not shake, so what else was there to worry about? Now at the beginning of my third year of school, I was starting to realize that my concentration could fail me. Getting tangled in the xylophone part in Bartok probably didn't happen because the percussionist's hands were shaking. The head can get rattled, too. Clearly, Inderal did nothing for my obsessive thoughts.

≀

That same year, 1985, Juilliard turned 80. To celebrate, the TV show *Live from Lincoln Center* was showcasing the school in a two-hour performance of drama, music, and dance. "Live" to the whole country, or at least anyone in the country who happened to watch PBS. It was *hyper*live. And I had a solo to play.

Warming up, I had a dialogue going with myself — one side took the position that what I was about to do was monumentally important, the other side minimized it. Right side saying, *I'm just accompanying the dancers, I'm playing in the pit, no one can even see me*; left saying, *It's running 16th notes on xylophone, it's a solo, if I freak out there will be a gaping silence on national TV*. It was just occurring to me that when you're playing from memory, you have to *remember* what you're playing. What if I had a memory slip?

As it turned out, I didn't have a memory slip. The performance was great, but the idea of *perfection* as the goal was settling into my head.

⁊

At that time, there was a perfect orchestral storm brewing. Symphony orchestras were in the big cities but now they were in small towns, too. Fort Worth, Jacksonville, Tulsa, Spokane — even these smaller orchestras were expanding. Seasons were getting longer, more musicians were entering music, the pay was rising. Yet programming for these orchestras remained extremely conservative. They played Beethoven and Brahms and Mozart, Schumann and Schubert, Prokofiev and Bartok and Shostakovich. White European and Russian male composers who wrote from about the mid-1700s to the 1950s. Everything else was an exception. The programmers would sandwich a contemporary piece after the overture and before the concerto, something written by a composer who was actually still alive, and then reward the audience with a big Mahler symphony after the intermission. Orchestras were becoming museums, taking a standard like Ravel's *Daphnis et Chloé* off its pedestal, polishing it for a live concert, placing it in storage for a few years, then putting it back into the lineup.

Not only was there a limited repertoire, but now the audience was listening to this music all the time. On portable CD players and in their cars. They heard the flute solo from *Daphnis et Chloé* with the Cleveland Orchestra on their way to work or they heard it with the Philadelphia Orchestra in their living rooms, so by the time the New York Philharmonic played it in a concert, the flute player had to recreate live what the other players had done in several takes. He was even competing with his own recordings.

It was these standard pieces that held the most terror. Playing Beethoven's Fifth Symphony? That was like being asked to paint the *Mona Lisa* while an audience watched. Make it perfect but at the same time make it *special*.

There was great relief in playing pieces that were not standards. Right after the *Live from Lincoln Center* concert, the Juilliard Contemporary Ensemble performed Messiaen's *From the Canyons to the Stars*. *Canyons* was a two-and-a-half-hour-long orchestral piece, and Caroline and I played the two solo parts — xylophone and bells. We stood between the first row of violins and the first row of the audience instead of hiding behind the brass like we usually did. Far more exposure, much more playing, yet I felt relaxed. It wasn't the kind of music an audience member would put on the CD player after a bad breakup. They wouldn't go home humming my part.

Conducting the Messiaen was Ethan Shipper. A violinist as well as a conductor, Ethan wore the same clothes every day: white button-down shirt, khaki pants, brown shoes. He had a brown tweed suit coat for coming and going. It looked like his silver frames could barely contain the business part of his glasses — they were the thickest I'd ever seen. His head was closely shaved, but the outline of his receding hairline was still visible, like a shadow. He was both bald and going bald at the same time.

One night we had a sectional — Ethan, Caroline, and me — along with the concertmaster and a piccolo player named Julie. This was my chance to study Ethan up close: the shadowy razor-stubble head, the grinning jaws full of crooked teeth, the delicate hands, and the long pale fingers. I watched him conduct and tried to imagine those hands in an ordinary act — changing a tire or mopping a floor. I couldn't.

We were set up in room 309, just the five of us surrounded by a hundred or so chairs from an earlier rehearsal. Like all of Messiaen's works, this one was filled with the sounds of birds — birdcalls in constantly changing meters and tempos. Messiaen's tempo markings were very precise: he spelled out the exact speed at which each of these passages was to be played. It was up to each musician to know the relationships between these passages — we had to do the math even before starting to practice. It was a fascinating puzzle.

Caroline was a natural at this. She had whole sections of xylophone solo with only light accompaniment. That night, without the orchestra playing, it was just the two of them — Ethan conducting, beating time through these changing patterns, and Caroline playing. She made it sound effortless, like she was improvising. Ethan was watching the score, smiling. A guy as smart as Ethan spent most of his life surrounded by people who were on lower rungs of the intelligence ladder than he. He was smiling at Caroline that night because she was his equal.

Then there was Julie. She was a flute player, a blonde, and a Texan. Three strikes. Ethan was quizzing her gently on the relationship between two bars — the end of one section and the beginning of the next. He laid it out for her: "I'm beating your groups of dotted 16ths."

She nodded.

"What happens to the tempo in the next measure?" he asked.

She giggled.

He seemed not surprised or annoyed that this was her answer. He waited patiently, hands and baton in his lap.

"Come on, Euclid," he said.

And Julie, in turn, seemed not surprised or annoyed that Ethan was insulting her, or maybe didn't know who Euclid was.

He gave her the answer, spelled it out for her, still smiling and rolling his eyes.

There was something charming about Ethan, although he certainly wasn't a regular guy. We cut a lot of slack for anyone who decided to become a musical dictator — demanding total compliance and waving a stick at us — but he wasn't even normal for a conductor.

Ethan would catch any mistakes I made. Still, a piece like the Messiaen released me from any *audience* expectations. Even someone who'd listened to it ahead of time would have trouble remembering what a crazed mockingbird would sing next. I could just show off.

♩

It was not a mystery as to why my anxiety was ramping up, why my honeymoon with Inderal was ending, why the seeming paradox that as my skills grew, as I became a better player, my nerves were getting worse — soon I would begin taking auditions. There was no formula for deciding when to start; in my self-directed little world, choosing when to put myself out there would be up to me. The only vague suggestion of when to begin had come from my Eastman precollege teacher. She made a comment about "wanting to get your third year behind you" before starting auditions. I took that as gospel.

Nothing begged the performer for perfection as much as an audition and — in my mind — no instrument more so than percussion. A trumpet player or a violinist could play out of tune, slightly too high or low. Snare drums and tambourine and triangle were all about rhythm and rhythms were math, and math was either right or wrong. Of course, the committee wanted a musical player and one who had a good concept of sound on all the instruments. But why not choose one from the vast crowd of percussionists who were also perfectionists?

Despite the angst it produced, having perfection as a goal was liberating. There was no ambiguity involved in this pursuit. This idea that perfection was attainable started to dribble into the few areas of my life that did not involve music. Perfection and control were concepts that could not be untangled. I began to follow the legions of other girls who dove into restricted eating, though I wouldn't go all the way to anorexia because that represented the ultimate loss of control: other people got involved and made you eat. Exerting control over food was simple. I'd already cut out meat; now I eliminated sugar, then dairy, then white flour. I was paring down, eliminating any excess, shaming the control freak I'd formerly been with my ability to control even more.

At the end of my second year, I'd given up my apartment — I no longer wanted to deal with the clutter and the roommates. Two whole rooms with a bathroom and kitchen suddenly seemed excessive. Juilliard had just formalized a relationship with the YMCA, and I moved in — $260 a month for a room and a closet. The entire room was about the size of a modern bathroom. There was one small window that looked nine stories down onto an alley. If I jumped, I would land in the dumpster.

Juilliard was paring down, too. The year before, we drummers had had a meeting with our new young president, laying out our frustrations for him — we had too many students for too few practice rooms; we were forced to practice in the hallways and stairwells. He agreed that there were too many students, although, for him, I think it had nothing to do with what the facilities could hold. A percussion department with 21 drummers? It made no sense to turn out that many players when there were so few jobs once we graduated. Through attrition and by accepting fewer players, we had only 12 drummers this year. Twelve still seemed far more than the world needed, especially since there were many other schools in the country churning out drummers. Still, it was an improvement.

As limited as the academic offerings were in which I had to participate, I was even dispatching with the last of those requirements this year. I chose The Bible as Literature because it was offered at the same time that Richard and Donald were both using their studios to teach, the worst time of the week for finding a place to practice. This class was my first real contact with the dancers at school. Not the elegant students of the School of American Ballet, who passed by our hall every day, goddesses with perfect posture, perfect bodies, perfect buns in their hair. These were the larger and smellier modern dancers. They came to class in leotards and T-shirts whose necklines they'd hacked up with scissors. They wore tights covered by crinkly warm-up pants. Some of them came barefoot. *Barefoot.* Their feet were among the most repulsive body parts I had ever seen and I couldn't take my eyes off them. Veined, corned, callused, bunioned — they slapped these feet on top of the desks in front of them. They brought food to class and ate constantly: nuts, baby carrots. One hulking girl with an Eleanor Roosevelt overbite brought in a red pepper and ate it like an apple. Our teacher was a professor at C. W. Post Campus on Long Island. There he taught real students. For us he decided it was probably more than enough just to learn some vocabulary. Every day he'd write words and phrases on the board. We'd copy them, then he'd read us passages that included them. *To know* was one. Followed by *To lay with.* Followed by *To go in unto.* Biblical euphemisms for sex would constitute my last non-musical education from Juilliard.

≀

The space shuttle *Challenger* exploded in January 1986, as the second half of my third year was beginning. Watching it blow up and divide into its twin trails made me wonder, in my self-absorbed way, about the engineers who had made such a colossal mistake and now were forced to relive their failure repeatedly on national television.

The musical equivalent of reliving a failure was recording. Making a recording was an exercise in perfectionistic torture — any mistake that was captured and slipped past the editing process would be stamped on a CD forever. Not only were you limited by time and money, but you had to try to make every take perfect because you weren't the only one playing. In *your* perfect take there could be a trumpet mistake. Your next perfect take — scratchy string sound. It felt like walking on eggshells, just hoping to keep getting it right.

March marked the one-year anniversary of the death of the composer Roger Sessions, and our new president decided to honor him by having Ethan Shipper and the Contemporary Ensemble record one of his works — *The Black Maskers Suite*. Sessions was famous in the tiny world of classical composers — he'd received several Guggenheim fellowships and a Pulitzer Prize, and had taught at the school for 18 years.

Most of us in the brass, winds, and percussion sections were well-prepared. With only one musician on each part, there was no one to cover any lack of preparedness. It was a group effort, but only in the final result. It was as if my wildest paranoid fantasies had come true — the editors, engineers, and musical assistants hunched over scores *were* all listening for any mistake we made.

It was different for the strings. There were no fewer than eight players playing each part. If one player had to fake a passage, few people would know. They contributed to the group, but there was not the same risk of exposure for them, not the same possibility of public humiliation.

But with no risk of humiliation, there was also no chance for glory. Having an orchestra made of string players of the highest caliber created both the world's most dazzling string section and also the most reluctant. They were required to play in an orchestra while at school but they didn't enjoy being buried in a crowd. Many believed they would add their names to a list that included Heifetz and Perlman and Casals and Ma; at the very least they hoped to become principals and concertmasters of the world's most impressive orchestras. Sometimes, when the concert came around, they would show off, and the result was stunning. I'd heard them play Tchaikovsky's piano concerto earlier that year. The piece begins with a section violin solo while the pianist just flops around playing chords. At the concert they unleashed their glorious sound, each playing as if they were the only one responsible for the soaring melody. It was like Beethoven's *Ode to Joy* sung by a chorus of Pavarottis and Sutherlands. Once these players left school, a lucky few would become soloists or play in quartets. Some would become concertmasters and some would play in a section or teach. Some would quit music. Wherever they might play in the future, they would never again play in a section surrounded by so much talent.

Also working against Ethan in this session was the fact that this was not only orchestral music, it was the much-dreaded contemporary music. *Contemptible* music. It required far more concentration than a Tchaikovsky melody. Ethan stopped to correct phrasing. He corrected dynamics. Most of his attention was directed at the violins — he reached for the concertmaster's violin and demonstrated. Time is limited in recording sessions, and as he stopped the orchestra repeatedly, the strings' attitude wore him down. In the end, it wasn't about ability. He needed, in this instance, to be more coach than teacher. If he had a section of average but hardworking players, he could have roused them with inspirational talk. For this group, the A-list varsity slackers, he reached for shame.

"You are going to have to learn to play in an orchestra," he told them. He adjusted his glasses as I'd seen him do many times now, gently pushing them back up on his nose with the delicate fingers of his left hand. He seemed, suddenly, to have nothing but time. "Sometimes you will even need to play contemporary music."

He put his chin down and peered over the top of his glasses at the whole of the violin section. "Not all of you are going to be running around the world playing the Whooziwhat concerto. Not all of you are going to be Izzys or Pinkys," he said, referring to Perlman and Zuckerman. "Most of you aren't even going to be *me*."

How we loved Ethan at that moment. We drummers and brass players in the back took a few precious and expensive moments of recording time to cheer our hero.

I was calmed throughout the session by the fact that this recording wasn't of a standard piece. At least my best takes couldn't be compared against a host of other best takes. I was now in the habit of pitting my anxiety-provoking situations against imaginary situations that were worse. That, for the moment, was my coping method.

10
Petty Tyrants

As he stands on the podium flailing his arms in the air, a conductor's job is both more and less than it appears. Some audience members give too much credit to the conductor, as if the baton itself issues forth sound in all the colors of the rainbow. The best conductors give a performance its shape; it is a collaborative effort between master and subjects, and we happily follow our fearless leader.

But far more frequently, we struggle to play well *in spite* of the conductor.

The conductor's performance would begin in rehearsals. Some were ingratiating, some stern; many had cavernous reservoirs of insecurity covered by bluster. Like a luxury watchmaker, he had to balance all the moving parts perfectly — *More here* to the flutes, *Don't drag* to the trumpets, so that the machine as a whole, *his* instrument, could tick with precision. Even before rehearsals, he spent time with the score, making fundamental choices about tempi, so as to faithfully interpret what the composer had written. But it went back even further than that — ideally he should know something about each instrument, their strengths and limitations, and should have played on the other side of the waving stick. He had to become the final arbiter of intonation; if, after a rehearsal or two, the players were themselves unable or unwilling to correct pitch issues, the conductor had to know what to do — *Violins, keep that D sharp a little lower*, or *Second trombone, you must come up in that chord*, or, more often than not, just an index finger pointed down to the stage or up to the ceiling. This was the work the audience didn't see. Rehearsals were the place in which the conductor did or didn't earn his money.

Sometimes a conductor was just technically bad. He didn't know it though. We could see him trying to work out the mystery in his head: he might give us terribly unclear gestures and then yell at us for not playing together; or he might move his arms faster, then yell at us for speeding up, forgetting that it's his foot on the gas pedal.

Whether good or bad, some conductors were just bat-shit crazy. That added a whole new level of interpretation for us. We were always trying to interpret their beat because that was our job. If a good conductor yelled, "You're behind!" I would play more energetically, more on top of the beat. But when they're crazy, we have to try to interpret their *personality*. I had to ask myself, is the idiot yelling "You're behind" because I'm behind? Is he trying to impress someone attending the rehearsal? Is he mad because there are two substitutes in the orchestra or because the guy playing principal cello plays relentlessly, aggressively flat? How much I adjust my anticipation of the beat depends on the answers to these questions.

By the night of the performance, most of the conductor's work is finished. At that point the conductor becomes a highly paid traffic cop — signaling tempi and meter to a hundred or so musicians. If one of his charges should miscount and enter incorrectly, he has to bring the wayward traveler back onto the main highway to fall in line with the rest of the cars. The rare occasions in which many musicians became derailed at once are the worst catastrophes of all — trainwrecks. The fault there is nearly always that of the conductor: so used to compliance, it was easy for the orchestra to blindly follow the stick-waver before realizing his moment of inattention had led us off a cliff.

Conductors, both good and bad, literally set the stage for the mood of the performance. Musically, the concert wasn't going to be much different from the last few rehearsals. All we needed at that point was clear technique and a smile or two of encouragement. Too often what we saw instead were constant Siskel-and-Ebert-type reactions on the conductor's face, a thumbs-up or thumbs-down expression for the whole orchestra to see. Most could not help scowling after something went wrong, a tactic which insured that by the musician's next entrance he's been primed with a needless layer of ass-puckering fear.

With a good conductor, we played our best. With a bad conductor, we played our best. Either way we colluded with the conductor against the audience; we never pulled back the curtain to expose the great and powerful Oz. At the end of the performance there were bows and smiles. Every day was Christmas — though sometimes it was the performance of a soon-to-be-divorced couple putting on a show so as not to ruin the holiday for the kids.

Our standards were high, and the few who exceeded them stood out. The great conductors were magical. Some had careers as instrumental soloists or were composers themselves. They didn't need to stop and discuss what they could show with the baton; they commanded the rehearsal with the stick.

During my first year of school, Leonard Bernstein had come to give a masterclass. The conducting students of the school were lined up against the wall of the rehearsal room, reviewing their scores, waiting for him to arrive. They would take turns leading the orchestra and Bernstein would critique them. He swept into the room, tan corduroy blazer draped over his shoulders like a cape. I had only ever seen him on album covers, where they usually showed him in profile: head tilted slightly back, eyes peering down his long nose and out over the orchestra. He had beautiful gray hair, lots of it. A line of teachers and administrators reached out to shake his hand and he, instead, pulled them in for a big hug.

Matthias, the best of the student conductors, began by leading the orchestra through the overture to Bizet's opera *Carmen*. Bernstein stopped him and asked about the tempo he was taking. Matthias had done his homework and was conducting at the same tempo Bernstein had taken on his famous Metropolitan Opera recording, a tempo the critics had labeled as untraditionally slow. Bernstein didn't want to be copied, though; he wanted to know the reason Matthias chose that tempo. "Because that's how fast the toreador walks as he enters the arena," Matthias said, and Bernstein smiled. Before Matthias began again, Bernstein talked about the moment of silence just before the repeat of the first section, about building the anticipation by making it just a little longer than it was supposed to be. By stretching that pause, holding your breath for that extra split second, you made sure the return of the melody felt like an explosion. When they moved on in the opera and were playing a section with overlapping woodwind melodies, he yelled out "Spain!" and somehow, with just that one word, the orchestra sounded different.

I would see Bernstein again in later years; by then he seemed less concerned about being taken seriously. He called the orchestra I was playing with "fan-fucking-tastic!" and referred to the tuba as "that big blow job." But that day at Juilliard, he was only thrilling.

James Nielsen was an example of a conductor from the other end of the spectrum. I crossed paths with him for five different concerts, an arc that took me from naive to slightly less naive.

James had some decent musical ideas but it seemed like he'd given up on fitting in socially. Maybe sometime during his high school years he'd decided that being written off as eccentric got him the least amount of negative attention. James was the music director of a New York freelance orchestra, the Jupiter Symphony, but he had previously been a bagman. His history with the school, at different times in his life, included both being a student and living in the park across the street. Moretti, Juilliard's associate dean, hadn't wanted to give him a concert with the school orchestra, but James had begged, and it was easy to imagine he was experienced at that.

He still looked a bit like a homeless person. At our first rehearsal, I studied him from the back of the orchestra. He was sitting on a stool at the podium, studying a score. His face sagged. His glasses were huge. With his chin pointed down, his eyes were hidden behind the thick top rims and I saw only his cheeks staring at me. Strands of slick gray hair fanned out over the top of his head.

Moretti came in and introduced James, as he did for the first rehearsal with every conductor, and we started with Tchaikovsky's Fourth Symphony. As James began, he was facing east toward Broadway. If room 309 had had windows instead of being sealed in the middle of the building like a bomb shelter, James would have been staring out at his former self, seated on a park bench looking in.

James was bad. "Little waltzes, little waltzes here," he called out in the first 9/8 section. He was trying too hard. He talked too much. What made it even harder for James was that we were overly familiar with the piece. Certain pieces were staples of youth orchestras everywhere — Dvorak's *New World Symphony*, Copland's *Hoedown*, Holst's *The Planets* — but the reigning king of these pieces was Tchaikovsky's Fourth. I would have been shocked if there was anyone at that rehearsal who hadn't played it before. At Interlochen, we even made up words to parts of the first movement, lyrics that referred to the camp founder's wife and her ability to conceive despite the reputed sterility of the founder.

It was almost never the case that a conductor would come into the first rehearsal, irritate the orchestra tremendously, make us question our desire to be in this profession, and then somehow turn things around and have some good rehearsals and a good concert. James was no exception. He irritated us, but he *infuriated* Moretti. Throughout the rehearsal period, he implored the associate dean for more time. Moretti said no. James asked for a sectional rehearsal, one involving just the winds.

Moretti said no. Well before the final dress rehearsal, we knew that James was about to have his debut and final concert with the Juilliard Orchestra on the same night.

The morning of the concert I made my usual stop at Sims for orange juice. Sims was manned by an army of ferocious Korean ladies whose only goal was to get you out of their deli. Their aggression thrilled me.

The cashier pounced on me, throwing my juice into a bag with a sapling's worth of napkins. Waste anything but time.

Swept efficiently out onto the sidewalk, I found myself standing in front of James.

"Ah had to tell you how much Ah've enjoyed your playing," he said. He pushed an index card into my hand. It was sweaty with hand grease. "This is my personnel manager's number." He backed up and at the same time stumbled forward, executing an unplanned bow. He caught himself and hurried away.

My mind was still on the Korean ladies' demonstration of supreme efficiency and took a minute to catch up. James was here at seven thirty in the morning? Had I ever seen him here before?

I looked at the card. It was just a woman's name and a phone number, no mention of the Jupiter Symphony. Usually it was the personnel manager who made the calls, hiring for each concert. Maybe he meant I should just call to tell her I was interested.

The Sims exit line was pushing at my back so I folded the card into my hand and crossed Columbus. It occurred to me I hadn't seen where James had gone. I'd been looking at the card when he disappeared, and now I looked carefully at the park as I passed it. He would know every tree, every bush in his former home.

To Moretti's great relief, we got through the concert that night and ended our involvement with James. The next morning I was back at Sims, standing in the chaos of the Saturday-morning crowd. There were too many non-regulars in their casual clothes. They didn't know the procedures and it drove the Korean ladies crazy. Someone was nudging into my space from behind; I countered by pushing the line forward. He nudged again. I turned around. It was James.

"Ah had to tell you again how much Ah enjoyed your playing," he said. He was wearing a knit hat and scarf, far too much clothing for the weather. "Ah had friends in the audience and they all commented on the cymbals." Even as he talked, he was backing away, eyes staring and wide through his glasses. "You are a fine player," he told me, and disappeared.

Even though I'd played an easy part, even though it was only one movement in one piece, I wanted to think James really liked my playing. When I told Sebastian about James telling me to call his personnel manager, the strange look he gave me opened the door for a reality check — wasn't a personnel manager supposed to call *me*? couldn't James have talked to me at rehearsal rather than follow me to a store? — but then the door slammed and my defenses settled back in around me and I decided that maybe James's friends had commented that the sounds coming from my direction had been the best ever fashioned from six pounds of metal. I could not pass up the experience of playing with a good freelance orchestra. I called the personnel manager and told her I would be interested in playing with the Jupiter Symphony.

꒜

That spring, she called me to play in their March subscription concert. It wasn't much — just the triangle part to Mozart's overture from *The Abduction from the Seraglio*. If I were to play it without the orchestra, it would sound like I'd gone crazy — the part consisted only of single quarter notes, one after the other, for five minutes. Put the triangle next to a suspect's ear and I could force a confession by the end of the piece.

At the first rehearsal, I made myself busy unpacking as the room filled up with the best of the New York freelance world. There were different types of freelancers in New York. One group did jobs like Westchester, jobs that took them out of the city for little pay to play with a mediocre orchestra. But the freelancers who played in Jupiter belonged to another group. These musicians played in the Orchestra of St. Luke's and the Orpheus Chamber Orchestra; they played in Carnegie and went on tour and made recordings. They were among the finest musicians in the country and stayed in New York because there they could play in great orchestras with other great musicians. I was in awe of them. They dated soap opera actresses. They picked up the *New York Times* on Saturday nights after work and slept late on Sundays. They lived in two-bedroom, rent-controlled apartments on Riverside. They yelled at inexperienced students. They scared me.

I fought with my insecure self, convinced I didn't belong in the same room as the great freelancers, then reminded myself I was only playing triangle and only on one piece, and at least my hands weren't going to shake because I'd taken Inderal. Finally rehearsal started, and I had to concentrate on James. We started the overture and I kept my eyes dutifully trained on him. I held the triangle so that its sides framed James from the waist up, and I played my quarter notes.

After an hour, James said he was done with the Mozart for the day and called an early break. I was relieved — I'd gotten through the first rehearsal and no one had yelled at me. I packed my triangle and triangle beaters. They were the most compact set of instruments I'd ever taken to a rehearsal. It was like being a flute player or, even better, a piccolo player. I zipped my knapsack and when I looked up, James was standing in front of me.

"You are the virtuoso of the triangle," he said. There was always an odd, forward-leaning motion within his body, so that now, even though his feet were fixed to the floor, I felt as though he were bearing down on me. I took a half step back and then noticed he was holding out his hand. After we shook, I looked down and saw that he had given me a twenty-dollar bill.

"Oh, no," I said, and laughed, trying to undo the rejection of saying no. I held it out, confused.

"You are the virtuoso of the triangle," he repeated, and put his clammy hand over mine.

"Oh," I said, "okay." I put the bill in my pocket.

For the rest of the week I left rehearsals quickly, taking the stairs rather than the elevator. By the time the concert was over, I had decided the best thing I could do was to spend the money in a smart way. I wanted to spend that particular 20 on something meaningful so that if I were ever to discover what exactly I had done to earn it, I would at least know I had used the money wisely. I went right from the concert in Alice Tully Hall to Tower Records and bought an album of Mahler's Ninth Symphony. And I chose to believe that James thought I played triangle better than he'd ever heard it played before.

After my coronation as the virtuoso of the triangle, I played two more concerts with the Jupiter Symphony. Both times I kept my distance from James. Then came my last concert with the orchestra, the one I didn't know was going to be my last.

The dress rehearsal was in Alice Tully the morning of the concert. James was stomping around on his podium, pitching a hissy fit. He wanted more rehearsal time, he was mad that people were talking and fooling around, he thought our break was too long. Between the last two pieces on the rehearsal we had a big percussion setup change. There wasn't enough room to leave all the instruments set up throughout the concert, so after playing the cello concerto we had to set up for two Strauss waltzes. During the concert, there would be time for this switch because James would be offstage, mopping his sweaty head with a towel. But for now he stood on the podium, short and pissy, glaring in our direction.

Feeling the pressure to hurry, I knocked over a music stand. Knocking over a music stand is never a small thing when there are instruments onstage that are worth as much as town houses. The orchestra gasped. The stand landed on the wood stage and resonated throughout the hall. The music came out of the folder, each piece floating on its own time to the floor.

"What is this histrionics going on back there?" James said.

I'd never heard the word before. *Histrionics.* I was taken with it. Was that a Southern thing? The second bassoon player had propped her bassoon in its holder and was trying to help me. I was still collecting the music and hadn't even picked up the stand.

"We're waiting for you," James said.

I tried to make up for it in the concert. Between the dress rehearsal and the concert, we choreographed our setup change. During the concert we completed the change, disaster-free, before James was ready to come back onstage.

After the concert I hung around backstage, thinking I might run into James and apologize for wasting time during the rehearsal. It was pointless — I knew I wouldn't be hired for Jupiter again. If my fit of clumsiness had happened during my first concert with James, he would probably have seen it as evidence of my virtuosic haste. I left Tully and walked home feeling bad. It was like a double negative: rejected, yet rejected by a person I didn't want attention from in the first place. Dumped by a guy who'd previously stalked me.

ƪ

I learned that work can be given and taken away, but it was a lesson I chose to believe was just about James, something peculiar to peculiar, formerly homeless men. James was strange; that wasn't normal behavior. And although he had the power to hire me or not for the Jupiter Symphony, it was only one orchestra. I didn't even want to freelance — I wanted to win an audition and have tenure. What I didn't ask myself: what if I had really wanted to freelance? What if it had been someone powerful, someone who could really affect my career? I didn't ask those questions because I didn't think that was a lesson I would need to learn.

11
Learning to Fail (aka Audition #1)

We would only have to step outside of our narrow world for a moment to see how ridiculous it was. We stood in corners and *hit* things. We tried to bang on things better than our colleagues did in order to win the chance to beat on things for a living. But why step out of this world? Normal people could make fun of us if they liked, but we were deadly serious.

Fate cooperated with my tidy, uptight life plan and presented me with my first audition just as my third year of school was ending. It was for the Metropolitan Opera Orchestra, and to take the audition I would only have to walk across the street from Juilliard.

We were, essentially, always preparing for auditions. Any improvements in my playing contributed to how well I would play at an audition. It would be a matter of getting the excerpts to sound great — the right notes, perfect rhythm, a little music and phrasing thrown in — and then to play them that way behind a screen when all I would really want to do is barf. And hope that my playing was better than anyone else's that day. The period right before an audition, from the time the orchestra sent out its list of required excerpts to the big day itself, was a time of hyper-focused practicing, and nothing — not talent, not drive, not dedication — served that time as well as a sub-clinical level of obsessive-compulsive disorder.

I was made for this kind of narrow focus. All the manifestations of obsessiveness were huge assets. The attention to detail, strict scheduling, unvarying routines, and planning paid off. Practice, critique, repeat. Repeat until perfect, which was impossible; therefore just repeat endlessly.

§

I was now living on 70th Street and Columbus Avenue. I had lasted at the YMCA for four months and then suddenly I couldn't stand it anymore. The showering and going to the bathroom and brushing my teeth with others. The drunk man I came upon one night, beached in the hallway. The radiator in my room that clanged. How could the passage of heat through pipes make a clanging noise? I'd given up having a kitchen but there were roaches everywhere. I fled. I now had my own sink, a half-sized refrigerator, and shared a bathroom with only three other "apartments" on my floor. (Only in New York could these rooms be called apartments — I had to unroll my single futon diagonally to fit it on the floor.) I didn't know who my floor mates were because we avoided each other. If I heard someone in the hall I would wait to use the bathroom. I didn't want to see what flesh had pressed the toilet seat before mine. They could've been serial killers — I had no idea. For me, it was perfect: $292 a month to live alone only four blocks from school.

Every morning in the six weeks before the audition, I reviewed my plan for the day as I walked those four blocks to school. It was the perfect time of year for an audition. Caroline was also taking it, and because the school cleared for the summer, she and I each had our own studio. Sebastian had gone home to his parents' house; I had no distractions.

Starting with xylophone, I warmed up. Scales, arpeggios, thirds, in every key, slowly, so as not to allow my muscle memory to memorize any wrong notes, and then faster.

By the time I finished warming up it would be about eight thirty. I started with Gershwin's *Porgy and Bess*, slowly.

8:31 — Play it again.

8:31:30 — Tape loop in my head says, *Bring out the accents more. Don't crescendo at the end, but don't diminuendo either.*

8:32 — Set the metronome to quarter note = 80. Play it again.

8:32–8:42 — Enter a metronomic trance. Play the excerpt, turn the metronome up a few points, play it again. My hands are fully involved, my head only minimally so, and my heart not at all, at least as far as "feeling" or "being moved by" the music is concerned.

8:42 — Achieve tempo quarter note = 132, the tempo the Met has specified. All applicants must learn it at this tempo.

8:43 — Play it again at 132.

8:43:30 — Play it again at 132. Miss a note. Say *fuck*.

8:44 — Calm down and play it again. Slowly.

93

8:45–2:00 — Repeat procedure with the other xylophone excerpts. Then bells. Then vibraphone, snare drum, tambourine, triangle, bass drum.

Sometime around two o'clock, Caroline and I would leave, together or separately, maybe eat lunch together, maybe sit in the park and talk about anything but music. Or we wouldn't talk, just watch the dogs and their walkers going by outside the fence or close our eyes and feel the sun on our faces.

In the late afternoon and evening I worked a little more, listening to recordings to hear the excerpts in context. All these steps took work and money. Go to Tower Records and buy the operas. Sit at home with an album on the turntable and put the needle down again and again, waiting to hear xylophone or bells or tambourine. Listen to the way it's played during the opera and how exposed the passage is. Mark down where it occurs — which side of the album and how far in — for repeated listening.

After a few weeks I started to record myself playing through the excerpts. I'd set up all the big instruments in Donald's studio — xylophone, bells, a table to hold my smaller instruments — then enter from the hallway carrying my snare drum, tambourine, triangle, cymbals, castanets, and mallets, all strategically tucked into bags slung over each shoulder or resting on top of my snare drum. I'd slowly lay out the instruments and mallets, then walk to the far side of the room to the table that held my recorder. Turning it on was the official start of each of these auditions — Sony Walkman as judge and jury. I'd play through the whole list once. Whether an excerpt went well or badly, there were no do-overs. Then at night I'd sit on my futon with my Walkman and headphones and critique myself. There with my pencil and paper, I became the committee and would catalog my notes-to-self. *Self* — *Don't forget the crescendo at the end of* Salome, *don't rush the first measure of* Porgy, *don't drag the first measure of* Porgy. *Start* Magic Flute *softer, end* Norma *louder. Take more time to settle sticks on the drum before starting "Carmelites." Breathe.*

I took a few lessons with Will, who had been at Eastman with me — he was in college while I was in pre-college. When I felt ready, I packed up my sticks and took the bus to New Jersey to play for Richard at his house.

{

New Jersey was brighter than New York; the sun didn't have to force its way through car exhaust and around buildings to reach the ground. I got off the bus, and Richard was waiting to drive me down the street to his house. It was always a shock to leave the city. Go to the suburbs, travel in a car — it felt like taking a field trip out of the asylum.

Richard's kind and grandmotherly wife, Jean, was waiting for us at their house. She made us lunch, which she ate with us, and then Richard and I headed to his basement studio.

His basement was small — what a real estate agent would upgrade to "cozy" — but really, any room looked small once it was crammed with percussion. Richard sat on a stool, the way he did during lessons at school, while I slid between xylophone and bells and snare drums, put music on stands, picked out mallets and sticks and tambourines.

I played through most of the excerpt list, which took

most of an hour. I had to play an excerpt, hear Richard's suggestion, try to fix the problem. Play it again.

When we were finished, I sat in a chair and started packing up, reaching for my wallet. When students took extra lessons from him he wouldn't charge more than $25 an hour, even though many teachers charged three or four times that. For this lesson, he refused to take any money at all.

Richard watched me from his stool. His hands were folded across his stomach. He was in no hurry. With a smile, he turned his head sideways to look at me.

"What are you going to do if you get the job?" he asked.

I didn't say anything. Winning my first professional audition seemed impossible. For all the students he'd had study with him, Richard didn't really understand auditions. In his day, auditions had been different. A position would open up in an orchestra because of a retirement or a death, and other members of the section would be called upon to suggest their best students for the job. Maybe the teacher would have two or three good students and they would all show up and play for the music director. That was it. The students who were picked were no less deserving than the current musicians who had to stand out in a crowd of 75 players. Orchestras were filled with incomparable talents who'd gotten their jobs decades before by simply playing for the music director. But our auditions were different.

Richard went on. "Will said you sounded good and all you needed to do was relax."

A thrill went through me, hearing that. I shut it down. I didn't need the pressure of anyone other than myself expecting me to do well.

This time period was pleasant — dumbly bumbling along, enjoying my progress and my afternoons off, feeling justified about the time off because the preparation I did in the morning was so hard and so concentrated. No muscle spasms, no daily panic attacks, no insomnia. I was inexperienced.

But all this satisfying order and obsessiveness and scheduled unscheduled time came to an end on the day of the audition. If in future auditions I would learn to start getting nervous weeks ahead of time, this first time it came all at once the moment I woke up that morning. My breathing was shallow. I stood up on my futon and, remembering Richard's advice about moving slowly and deliberately, I walked the two steps to my sink and slowly picked up my toothbrush. It flew out of my hand and landed on the floor. I decided I would do exactly the opposite. I needed to move so fast that the racing of my heart matched the speed of my hands. Otherwise, I would have to see how much they were shaking.

Warming up at school, I decided to take my pulse. I had some idea that this would help me feel in control. I would be my own doctor and clinically decide how much Inderal I would need based on my heart rate. My pulse was 180. Either I was too nervous to count correctly or I had turned into a hummingbird. I took 40 milligrams of Inderal, which was the amount my doctor had told me to take. I packed my instruments, and headed for the elevator.

Caroline had been at school an hour earlier, warming up. We had agreed to walk over together, to march to the scaffold as a pair, but when I looked for her on the way out, she had already left. This was something we had to do alone. I walked in front of Juilliard, across 65th Street, and into the underground entrance of the Met.

At this point, ideally, I would be like an athlete. Focused with that stare Olympic gymnast Mary Lou Retton had when she was about to vault for the gold. When I was 16 and getting ready to play a concerto in front of an orchestra and an audience, I did feel like that. Now, however, I was numb.

In my own warm-up room at the Met, I unpacked my sticks and took my pulse again. One-twenty. I took another 20 milligrams of Inderal.

A monitor came for me and asked if I was ready. I was afraid but unable to show it: mentally buzzing, physically blunted. Ready.

The monitor led me down a hall and opened the door onto a small stage. It was set up with instruments lined up in two rows, each with its own music stand. At the edge of the stage there was a wall of folding screens. Behind this wall sat the committee. I could hear their soft noises as they whispered, sipped coffee, put pencils down on the table. I had no idea who was there. Orchestras usually formed a committee consisting of section members of the same instrument — percussionists for a percussion opening, violinists for a violin opening — then filled it out with musicians from other sections.

To the committee I was just number seven. I was genderless, ageless, raceless, with no school affiliation and no voice. As I arranged my sticks and smaller instruments on a table, the monitor reminded me not to talk. If I had a question, I was to motion to her, then whisper in her ear. She said I would start on xylophone with *Porgy and Bess*.

Now that the Inderal was working, I was able to follow Richard's advice. In slow motion I removed my *Porgy* mallets from my stick bag and faced the music. This was out of habit — after thousands of repetitions, all these excerpts had long been memorized. The monitor turned on the metronome to give me the tempo, then turned it off.

Then: silence.

Puncturing that silence felt like standing on a pew in church and screaming "fuck."

It was not a complete disaster. I started at the tempo she gave me and I didn't speed up or slow down (two of the worst offenses), but in one awkward passage, I stumbled. Tripping on my own mallets, I played several wrong notes. One of the biggest obstacles in percussion auditions was that we were playing on unfamiliar mallet instruments. It was fair — we were all equally disadvantaged — but disturbing when all other aspects of our preparation could be so rigidly controlled.

After that mistake, I went ahead and made the rest of the common mistakes, ones I had been warned about but needed to learn myself. Someone on the committee asked me to play *Porgy* again. Although this time it was better, I still committed two sins: I concentrated on the mistakes I'd made in the first run-through, and I assumed that every mistake I'd made had been noticed by the committee. Nameless, Faceless Committee Member may have actually asked me to play it again because he thought it was basically good but wanted to see if I could do it better. More likely he'd accidentally drifted off or spilled coffee and wasn't sure how I'd played it. The percussionists on the other side of the screen knew the excerpts well, but there were brass and wind and string players over there, too, who weren't as familiar with them.

Playing Mozart's *Magic Flute* on bells, I committed a third sin, thinking that if an excerpt wasn't "perfect" (the goal in all those hours of practicing) then it didn't count and showed only that I sucked. Actually, I did kind of suck. But instead of trying to recover, I spiraled down, caught for the remaining five minutes in a final sin, that of cataloguing my sins, trying to salvage this as a learning experience for future auditions but not bothering to wait until I was out the door.

Later I learned that I'd gotten two votes. Two of seven committee members thought I'd played well enough to pass to the semifinals and play again. I had needed four votes to move on.

After the audition, Caroline and I were back in our spot. It was the same spot in the park, and the same sun, but now I was drinking a beer in a bag, toasting and con-gratulating Caroline, who was not drinking because she had to keep practicing for the semifinals, which were in two days. Caroline had gotten through to the next round; I hadn't. I had already cried in the bathroom at the Met. There would be more crying later, but for the moment I was just feeling relieved, feeling the incredible change in pressure from this morning. I had the bends. And from the Inderal, a headache.

After three days and three rounds, they narrowed the field down to one drummer. A guy who'd gone to Temple University and spent a few years playing in a smaller orchestra was offered the job.

&

Now that I had taken my first audition, I was ready for more. I hadn't won the job, I hadn't even made it to the next round, but I kept in mind the other things I hadn't done: collapsed on the floor in a heap from fright, taken an overdose of Inderal, played an excerpt so badly the committee couldn't have guessed which excerpt it was. All of the parts of the audition that were under my control had gone reasonably well.

There were always going to be parts that were not under my control. Once I had learned to do all I could do, luck entered the picture to take care of the rest. There was the question of style — an orchestra might prefer darker-sounding cymbals over bright ones, snare-drum sounds that were tight and crisp or deep and throaty. There were so many other factors: playing first, playing last, playing after someone who had just played great; committee members who were hungry or tired, who had just eaten lunch, or who were waiting for lunch; having sweaty hands, cold hands, hands drained of blood because all the blood was up at chest level trying to keep my heart beating.

That there were factors outside of my control only added another level of crazy to my thinking about auditions. I would have to squeeze harder on the factors that were within my control to minimize the effect of those that were not.

≀

After the audition, I had nothing to do for the summer. I had auditioned for Tanglewood and was put on the waiting list. I had no backup festival. Getting that rejection letter terrified me. I needed to go to Tanglewood, needed the experience, needed to be around competitors all summer, especially ones from other schools. Of course,

I could get in next year or the year after that; all that experience and competition would still be available. But the one thing that wasn't available was following exactly in Caroline's footsteps — Colorado after the second year, Tanglewood after the third. My failure there was devastating to me.

I had no reason to stay in New York. I sublet my apartment for the summer so I could live more cheaply with my parents. Back home in Rochester, I practiced. I found myself a part-time job doing inventory work at Sibley's department store, working with the assistant buyer for the "stuff" department. Deb and I worked side by side counting glass animal figurines. I wondered why she was stuck doing this job, and it would make my head swim in fear. If I didn't win an audition, I would have to get a job even worse than hers. She came in every morning with perfect hair and in her upstate New York accent would say, "Good morning, *Pay*-ot," and then begin the day's duties of caring about the shit that people bought to fill their living spaces. I imagined her life picking out the vases and the fake plants we were inventorying, and when she came in one day beaming and telling me that she and her husband had bought a condo, I spent the rest of my working time imagining her life in fast forward: buying furniture for her new place, cluttering it up with crap she brought home from work, having a baby, then another, getting a divorce, getting remarried, dramas, boredom, death.

I'd go home to my parents' basement and practice harder.

⁊

When I had first gotten home, I wrote thank-you letters to Richard and to Will for helping me with the audition. A week after I'd finished the inventory job, I was sitting at the kitchen table reading the paper. Eating lunch and taking a break from practicing, I'd opened the sliding glass door to get some air. The basement had small prison-cell windows set high on the wall and I needed to see the sun before heading back down there. My mom was at the front door getting the mail. When she came into the kitchen she handed me a letter. It was from Richard.

I really appreciate what you said in your letter, he had written. He said he was glad to have helped. He thought I had prepared well and would use what I'd learned for the next audition.

I tried to remember the letter I had written him. His and Will's were nearly identical: *Thank you for your help, I'm disappointed but learned a lot, I will continue to work hard*. I did remember using small note cards because I knew I didn't have much to say and writing them side by side, copying what I wrote except for the names. Sincere but efficient. Will had written nothing; Richard had written a thank-you note for a thank-you note. I put it back into the envelope, folded it a few times, and shoved it down into the trash.

12
Lesson

In my first year of playing percussion, I learned an important lesson: relationships between you and other drummers could affect your musical life. In fifth grade, the lesson went like this: My section in band consisted of four boys and me. One of them was in sixth grade and was in charge of assigning the best parts (snare drum) to himself and the boring parts (triangle) to the rest of us.

One Saturday, my friend Ann and I were at the skating rink. We had three unsupervised hours to track the movements of a group of boys from our school, a group that included my drummer-section mate, who was Ann's boyfriend. Chasing boys was what we did in fifth grade. I went along with it but wasn't quite interested yet. The closest I'd gotten was being "asked out" by Ricky Meyer. I told him no. He told me to go fuck myself up a tree.

One of the obligations of "going out," apparently, was that you had to make out with your boyfriend. Publicly. After about an hour of skating, a posse of sixth-grade girls approached Ann. There was a small room at the back of the rink, they told her. It was used as a changing room for kids who took private lessons. Meet your boyfriend there in five minutes, they said. I followed her. I realized that if I climbed to the top of the bleachers next to this makeshift changing room, I could see over the wall. A crowd of boys sat behind me.

The word was they were "going to third." Third was French-kissing and *feeling down*. Even then I wondered how the person who had developed that rating system could have put them on the same base. I was horrified by both, but still thought that touching tongues was something that should come way before touching a crotch.

Down below, Ann and her boyfriend sat on a bench. If his parents could've foreseen such a situation — fluorescent lights, onlookers, arms locked around his younger girlfriend — maybe they wouldn't have given him the name they did.

His actual name? Harry Bliss.

Two boys entered the room and approached Harry and Ann, clumping across the black rubber floor in their skates. They instructed the pair to kiss. And kiss again. I leaned over, trying to see if they were using their tongues. After the second kiss, the boys didn't know what to do. Kiss again, they said, and left the room. Ann and Harry kissed, just a peck this time, and the boys behind me cheered. Harry looked up, startled.

The show over, I climbed down and stood in front of the door. A line formed behind me, like autograph seekers. Ann came out first, Harry slinking behind her. Both were blushing fiercely. Ann looked embarrassed but smiled at the crowd of onlookers, showing us the wide gaps in her upper teeth.

Harry was not embarrassed, he was mad. As he

walked past me, hockey skates bent in at the ankles, he held a finger close to my face and shook it.

"You're never playing snare drum or bass drum again!" he said.

My turn to fiercely blush. What had I actually done wrong? Eventually, I would realize young Harry lacked the power or maybe the desire to carry out his threat. But at the time, the lesson I learned was more specific than global: *Don't watch the leader of your section kiss his girlfriend because you'll be stuck playing triangle for the rest of your life.* So noted.

Anyone who has ever studied music knows that lessons are learned through repetition.

♩

When I got around to watching the "Juilliard at 80" program we had recorded for *Live from Lincoln Center* on PBS, I saw they had included text at the beginning of one of the segments. It said, "The heart of Juilliard is one-on-one instruction." It was true, but it wasn't unique to Juilliard — it was unique to music. Even dance and drama were taught in classes, but at every music conservatory around the world, learning to play an instrument was a process undertaken by student and teacher, alone in a room for an hour a week. That was enough to sum up the relationships we had with our teachers. It wasn't about our *teachers*, plural, those who stood in front of a classroom and wrote composers' names and dates on the board while we ignored them. It was about our *teacher*. We spent an hour a week with the one person to whom we entrusted our musical education, grinding out that glacial process of improvement.

Overstating the importance of this relationship would be impossible. Your teacher could write recommendations for summer festivals. Or if an audition was being held and they were only inviting certain people — no cattle call — a word from your teacher to a teacher who played in that orchestra might get you in.

It wasn't just calls or recommendation letters. A teacher could teach you everything he knew. Incrementally, week by week, over the course of years, knowledge was passed from him to you. Or not. He could spend the hour of your lesson saying you sounded great, blowing smoke up your ass. Teaching you nothing.

As I waited outside Richard's studio, about to have a lesson at the end of September of my fourth year of school, I was preoccupied with what might be wrong with him. Since the beginning of the school year, Richard hadn't been himself. He wasn't smiling, he wasn't saying much in lessons, he got tongue-tied and frustrated a few times when trying to offer corrections. We weren't used to this.

Sharon had the lesson before mine. Knowing I was the last lesson of the day, she and I had talked about the possibility of taking Richard out to dinner, maybe cheering him up. So after I'd suffered through a nearly silent hour with him, during which I asked him question after question just to get him to talk, Sharon stuck her head into the room and said we were going out. Richard agreed to come.

We took him to the Lincoln Square Coffee Shop, a diner across the street from school, fluorescently lit and loud. Most people there were overdressed for such a place; they were eating before going to a concert or the opera. We all ordered our food, and Sharon and I ate

107

while Richard sat and said nothing. His grilled cheese congealed in front of him, sweating grease. He answered our questions but volunteered nothing else.

I think I felt, at this point, that our teachers were like our parents: they worked out their own problems themselves. There wasn't much for us to do or worry about — we couldn't solve their issues. I'd already started thinking about what I needed to practice that night and was getting anxious just sitting there. Sharon had to meet someone at six and got up to leave. I ordered dessert and, still cheery, still pretending this was just an ordinary dinner and Richard wasn't moping, said I would keep him company.

Eating my dessert, I babbled at him. Thinking I could at least distract him from his problems, I talked about snare drums, about the trouble I was having finding one that worked well for soft playing. I couldn't tell if Richard was listening. He had pushed his sandwich aside and had his hands resting on the table, folded.

When I was ready to go, Richard lifted his head and heaved a sigh so dramatic it seemed like an invitation to ask him a question.

I did. "Is something wrong, Richard?"

"I never meant to fall in love with you," he said.

My jaw came unhinged and dropped.

"You're letting the flies in," Richard said. And finally, for the first time I'd seen in weeks, he smiled.

❧

After dinner, I practiced. I didn't think about what Richard had just told me; instead I played snare drum. Early in the fall was a great time for really learning — not consolidating to get ready for summer festival auditions, not preparing for ensemble performances — just taking what I did least well, examining it, and making it better. But while I was practicing this night I was also learning to ignore what wasn't convenient. Learning to ignore this revelation of Richard's that had the potential to derail me, to repress it so completely that it went underground and only came to the surface as anxiety.

The only thing I said to him that night was "I'll do anything I can to help." It was as if he had just told me he had cancer; that was how bad the news sounded. This terrible thing had happened and I would do anything I could to help him get over it. I assumed he saw the situation as I did — these feelings had come to him and he made a mistake in telling me about them. He would regret his revelation. We'd never talk about it again.

The next day, a Wednesday, I was practicing xylophone in front of the orchestra library when Richard suddenly appeared next to me. He looked radiant. Gone was the sagging face from the last several weeks — now he was nearly glowing.

"What brings you here?" I asked. His teaching days were Tuesday and Thursday.

"I wanted to give you something." He reached into his stick bag, a black two-handled bag like a TV doctor's, and handed me a bright yellow envelope. He had just come from outside, still dressed in his raincoat and cap, the turquoise stone of his bolo tie showing at his neck. He shuffled the few steps over to the bench and sat. As usual, when Richard appeared at school, he attracted a few drummers and soon he was chatting, cheerfully holding court. I slipped the envelope behind the music on my stand.

Alone in my apartment that night, I opened it. Squinting, I skimmed it, trying not to see too much. He told me again of his feelings for me. Nearly every sentence ended in an exclamation point. Some had two or three.

I threw the letter away and left my apartment.

Out on the street it was a beautiful night. I walked across 70th, passing the skinny trees that lined all the side streets. In the suburbs it was the houses that were surrounded by fences, here it was the trees. Each was its own island in concrete. At Central Park West, I turned left. It felt suburban over here. There were no stores or restaurants. Most of the people out on the sidewalk were coming home late from work or taking their dogs out. I passed the Dakota at 72nd Street. John Lennon had been shot there, right outside the guards' shack. I walked past the Langham on the next block, where Mia Farrow lived with her many children, then turned left on 74th Street, where Sebastian lived, just in from the park.

Sebastian's apartment was a floor above the sidewalk. In another city, his building would've looked like public housing: plain brick front and below-street-level entryway crowded with garbage cans, menus littering the doorway under a sign that said *No Menues*, a word whose spelling no one in New York could agree on. But placed here, steps from the park, it was a pricey, desirable apartment.

Sebastian and Dennis and I sat at their tiny kitchen table, listening to Mahler's Fifth Symphony. I thought about Richard's letter.

Sebastian and I spent most of our time in the same building, yet still alone. When we were together we had beers, we listened to music, we laughed and acted like we might still be in fifth grade. I never would've thought to tell him about what had happened with Richard. So much was already unspoken between us; we didn't talk about our dreams because we had the same ones.

And there was certainly no reason to say something about Richard now. I assumed it was done. We would go back to having our lessons, teacher and student, and he would never talk about it again.

I was wrong. After my next lesson the following Tuesday, Richard said, "Let's go to dinner," and we went. After we'd gone to dinner twice, it was a routine, and once it was a routine, it became something I would have to actively opt out of. If I didn't go, I would have to admit to myself that there was something uncomfortable about it — we were going on what felt very much like a date every week. If I continued to go, it was because there was nothing wrong with having dinner with my teacher every week. Every other week, I made sure to pick up the check. For me, optimism and denial were not so far apart.

There was another reason to act like nothing was wrong — something that came back to me from my first year at school. I'd been waiting for a lesson with Richard one Tuesday afternoon, standing in the hallway by the lockers. An orchestra rehearsal was about to start, so the hall was crowded with bass players who had to open their big locker doors and maneuver their instruments down the hall and into room 309. Caroline and I were talking to a girl named Kathy, a drummer who'd finished school and had stayed in town to freelance. It was the first time we'd met, but I knew a little about her. I knew she was older and she didn't have a mean bone in her body. And I knew Richard never referred to her by name. He called her "the Princess." As we were talking, Richard had been making his way through the bass players. We didn't notice him until he was next to us.

Kathy seemed surprised. She probably hadn't seen him since she'd graduated. "Richard, how *are* you?"

"Fine," he said, unsmiling, and then he did a strange thing. Despite the crowd and the wide hall, despite Kathy's petite size and the fact that Richard didn't really have a sideways, he turned his back to the lockers and squeezed against them to shuffle past Kathy.

I asked Caroline why Richard, who was nice to every-body, didn't like Kathy.

"She switched teachers without telling him," Caroline said. Kathy had decided to study with one of the other teachers and officially changed. This wasn't unusual — drummers were the exception to the "one teacher" rule because our teachers had their own specialties among the many instruments we had to cover. For string players or pianists, switching teachers was like getting a divorce. There were egos involved, and it didn't happen often. But even when we drummers did it, it was discussed and decided upon with whomever you were currently studying.

I asked Caroline why Kathy had done it, but she didn't know.

Now I thought I might have an idea why. This was a lesson from Kathy. Maybe Richard had said, *Practice this, play it this way, take this tempo, I love you, let's go to dinner.* Maybe Kathy had found herself in that situ-ation, wanted out, and switched teachers. And for that, she'd been exiled. I didn't know if it was true or not, but I didn't need to know — it guided my decisions and non-decisions as surely as if she'd confirmed it for me.

}

My lesson ended at five or sometimes five ten, five fif-
teen — I always had more to play, more questions to ask.
Then I took my instruments, sticks, and music back to my
locker while Richard packed up and locked his cabinet.
I imagined that because mine was the last lesson of the
day, it looked as if I was just keeping Richard company.
We went to the Lincoln Square Coffee Shop, though as
the weeks went on he began to lobby for another, any
other, restaurant. Once we went to Fiorello's, once to
Houlihan's — each was more of a real restaurant, with
dim lighting and less-hurried service. I continued to praise
the coffee shop and claimed it was my favorite. Richard
would sigh and shake his head, but soon he didn't ask
to go anywhere else, and I could count on the fact that
at least we would be sitting in the fluorescent light and
wouldn't have to walk more than two blocks to get there.

During dinner I talked nonstop — about snare drums,
excerpts, conductors, summer festival auditions — and
Richard listened and smiled at me, and when I said something he thought was naive he'd laugh. He'd begun making
me tapes of albums from his jazz collection, and at some
point during dinner he'd hand me the latest installment.
In a casual conversation the year before, I'd mentioned
that I didn't like jazz, didn't understand it. That wasn't
even true. I liked Gary Burton and Chick Corea, Michel
Camilo, Paquito D'Rivera; I just didn't like the big bands
from Richard's era. Jazz confused me — it was wild and
untamed, and I was nothing if not a rigid, rote-learning
control freak. The tapes were labeled *The Patti Niemi
Home Study Course in Jazz Appreciation*. Tape number
one was of the pianist Roger Kellaway, and on the liner
notes, after listing the names of the songs, Richard had
written that Kellaway's music "somehow reminds me of

you!" I listened to that tape, the whole thing, afraid he might have recorded a message among the tracks and would later quiz me to make sure I'd heard it. The next one I skimmed, fast-forwarding to the end of each track, and after that they began to pile up, unlistened to, a stack of them on the floor of my closet.

As soon as the plates were cleared, Richard would begin rearranging the table — parting the salt and pepper shakers, one to each side, pushing the dispenser of sugar packets to the corner. In between, he placed the backs of his hands on the table, facing up, and curled his fingers to ask for my hands. I had seen a sea anemone once, and Richard's fingers reminded me of it, how its tendrils waved back and forth, back and forth, searching for food. There we would sit, hands to moist hands, white noise filling my head, and Richard would massage my fingers and look at me with a smile that, as the fall went on, reached less and less high up his cheeks. He'd tell me he loved me and I would look down at the table. I never said anything.

꠸

I told no one. If I'd articulated the situation to someone, it would've been transformed from some vague under-standing I had of Richard's feelings to concrete facts I then couldn't ignore. And even if I'd wanted to share this information, I didn't have an outlet for it. Caroline was my best friend — Sebastian was my boyfriend. Richard was their teacher, too. Richard's outlet was his shrink. He talked about me — he said he even brought in pictures of me to show the therapist. Sometimes it made me wonder how the therapist responded when he heard that Richard had taken me to dinner, told me he loved me, and told me

I was the first thing on his mind when he woke up and the last thing before he went to sleep.

Maybe it *wasn't* wrong. I didn't know. I understood Richard's declaration as well as I understood how a car's engine worked. I knew that as the months of that year wore on, there were many times I would wake up with a queasiness, feeling like I'd been drinking the night before even when I hadn't.

There was another reason I was confused: Richard didn't seem to think anything about this was bad. I never thought he *intended* to cause me any anxiety. So much went on behind those Juilliard studio doors: behavior running from physical to emotional; true to embellished to invented; forced, coerced, to mutually pursued. But whatever went on, no one talked about it. If no one told Richard it was wrong, was it wrong?

That was one of the questions I was not thinking about. If I had thought about them, I'd have to admit I had no answers. Richard was in love with me? What did that mean? What did he hope would happen when he told me?

Since I believed he didn't mean to cause me harm, I wasn't mad at him, just desperately anxious. The only person I was mad at was myself for not knowing what to do.

13
Stage Fright, Part III:
Constant Low-Grade Fear
(with acute flare-ups)

If I'd been able to imagine it was possible to have more anxiety, I would have camped under my xylophone in my parents' basement and refused to come back to school. But anxiety made no allowances for what I had the capacity to endure. It showed up at the door, and my choice was to let it in or flee. Leaving music was not an option. So I opened the door to this situation with Richard and allowed it to mingle with the crowd.

This was supposed to be my last year of school, and most of the anxiety was still about the math: how many orchestras divided by how many percussionists. Caroline was a year ahead of me and was now doing a fifth year, after which she would have a master's degree as well as a bachelor's. I knew that would be a realistic option for me, too, but the feeling had already begun to creep in — *You're at Juilliard, now it's time to get out.*

With no natural light in the hallways or studios, September became October and then November seamlessly. When I walked to school it was gray outside; when I went out to get a sandwich for lunch it was gray outside. By dinnertime it was dark.

There was little that fall that I would call comic relief, but one day in November a call came into Associate Dean Moretti's office from a producer at *The Today Show*. In a few weeks they would be taping their Christmas special. Most of their shows were broadcast live, but Christmas was taped ahead of time so their workers could have the day off. Their vague idea, which they needed help in fleshing out, was to have some percussionists play some kind of holiday music on some kind of instruments. Moretti gave the assignment to Sebastian, who asked another drummer, Gary, and me to play with him.

We decided to stun the Christmas-morning television audience by playing "Jingle Bells" on marimbas. We would invite "the talent" (which was how they referred to those who were actually in front of the cameras, as opposed to those working behind the scenes) to accompany us on sleigh bells.

At five o'clock on the morning of the taping we arrived at Rockefeller Center, courtesy of a limo that NBC had sent to pick us up in front of Sebastian's walk-up. It was so early, there were no gawkers to see how casual we could be about the whole thing: limo, chauffeur opening the door for us, star treatment. We were talent for a day. Once in the lobby, we were escorted past a line of tourists waiting for a studio tour.

Our marimbas had been set up in front of a wall-sized picture of the New York skyline. Lit from behind, it was supposed to look like we were playing in front of a large window. Across from us were the couches and coffee table where they interviewed guests. Sebastian, Gary, and I stood off to the side of the set, waiting. Crew members walked around with headsets on, holding clipboards and ignoring us.

We had time to rehearse "Jingle Bells" just once before they had to get ready for that day's live show. We were sent to get made up with a full-face pancake and then we were on our own until they called for us.

No one said how long that would be. We stood in a hallway and watched people. Some heavily made-up faces stood out. Comic Steve Martin and actress Veronica Hamel stood next to each other, waiting to be led somewhere by someone. TV host Bryant Gumbel walked by. "Happy fucking Christmas!" he said to whomever was listening. It appeared that Sebastian and I were the only ones listening, which was probably why he was in such a bad mood. Around noon we discovered the buffet. Willard Scott, *The Today Show*'s weatherman, was in line. Having met me earlier that morning in rehearsal, he greeted me like we were buddies. "This is the love of my life!" he told the room, putting his hands on my shoulders. No one cared. After a few more hours of wandering, we ended up in the greenroom. Actor Hal Linden was there, waiting to tape his segment. Singer James Taylor came in and sat down, and we were too intimidated to say more than hello. He said hi and then started doing some paperwork in his lap. It looked like he was paying bills.

Eleven hours after we had arrived, we were finally called back to the studio. While we had been wandering and trying to keep busy, the cast and crew had already put in a long day's work. They started taping immediately. Bryant introduced us to the future Christmas audience.

"The percussion group from the famed Juilliard School of Music, which trains future symphony orchestra musicians, will bring us their unique interpretation of 'Jingle Bells,'" he announced, while we stood in a line next to him, looking dull. "Now, you're going to do it on marimbas. The equipment you've got here, are they a normal part of a symphony orchestra?" He directed this to Gary.

"Um, yes they are," Gary said. "They're all, uh, you could find them in an orchestra, most of the time. They may not be used frequently, but, uh, we're responsible for knowing how to play all of them."

"Uh-huh," said Bryant. And to me: "What about some of these other little goodies you've brought along? I mean, are those part of the equipment, too, including this little jobbie —" he smacked a temple block with his hand "— that I've been practicing for about a month?"

I laughed, kind of. It sounded more like a burp. "Yeah, those are temple blocks," I said, "and, uh, rarely you'd find them in an orchestra, but you would find them, along with a lot of other sound effects."

We knew too much about our subject and it made us sound stupid. The long explanation would have been that while you might find marimba scored for in some contemporary orchestral piece and temple blocks in Ferde Grofé's *Grand Canyon Suite*, and the sleigh bells we were about to use to excess were beautifully scored for in Mahler's Fourth Symphony, these particular instruments were used most often in bad holiday music. Gary and I were trying to be accurate. Would we use them in an orchestra? Uh, yes but no. We were bad TV. Bad talent.

Bryant, who was good TV and knew a little about a lot, turned to Sebastian. "Then what happens?" he asked. "Do you get immediate placement somewhere?"

"Oh, no," Sebastian said.

"No?"

"Auditions for major symphony orchestras."

"Let's bring the bozos in," Bryant said.

The talent came onstage: Jane Pauley, Gene Shalit, John Palmer, and Willard Scott. "Good evening, ma'am," Willard said to me. He kissed my hand.

"What's Willard got," Bryant said, "besides her hand?"

"A duck call," Gary said, and introduced the rest of the instruments. John had a set of sleigh bells, Gene a slide whistle, Bryant the temple blocks. Jane had a mouth siren and a heavy set of sleigh bells fixed to a strap and slung over her shoulder.

We started to play. Gene, John, and Willard ignored the lesson we had given them in rehearsal and played whenever they felt like it. Jane tried to shake the bells when she could. She had to lean sideways to keep the strap on her shoulder but she kept smiling. Bryant, who followed our instructions to play only during the chorus, danced while he waited. That is, he bent his arms at the elbows and twisted his upper body, like the gopher in *Caddyshack*. I imagined him at home on Christmas Day, watching the segment and drinking heavily.

Twelve hours after we arrived, we were done. We went back to the greenroom, collected our coats, and put away our mallets. Hal Linden was still there. I think the fact that a much bigger star, James Taylor, had been around all afternoon made him feel small. To compensate, he was demanding that the assistant get him a car to take him to his play. "So sorry," she told us — she had assumed he wasn't going to need one because the theater was only a block and a half away. But no matter. She gave him ours and told us to take a cab. We were talent no longer.

{

The only obligation I had left before going home for the Christmas break was my Music History II final. The class was taught by Patrick Moss, a man who seemed at odds with his own body. He had a combover that began just above his left ear, then fanned out in copper brown over the top of his head until it reached his right ear. As he sat in his chair in front of the class, some tightly wound inner anxiety forced him to constantly reposition his legs so they lined up perfectly side by side, and then place a palm on each knee.

It was Mr. Moss's job to cover a segment of the history of music, the part that involved white European and American men from about the 17th century up to the still-living Aaron Copland. We had to memorize facts like "the *Fitzwilliam Virginal* is a collection of 197 English keyboard pieces," and identify which symphony or opera or concerto we were hearing when Mr. Moss stood over the turntable, hand trembling, and placed the needle on the record.

Fortunately, Sebastian's roommate Dennis was in my class. The year before, in Music History I, we had developed a successful method of studying and planned on repeating it. Our method consisted of meeting at the fifth-floor elevators the night before the test. It was eight thirty, an hour and a half before school closed for the night, late enough that the classrooms and offices were quiet. The only activity came from the library.

Dennis and I walked away from the library toward the other side of the building. We were in a long hall, one that ran the length of the school along 66th Street. The hall was completely empty. Dennis took his master key from his pocket — we all had copies of this key — and let us into Mr. Moss's office.

I turned the light on. The office was one of many surrounding an empty concrete courtyard; nobody seemed to have the time or the vision to make the courtyard beautiful. Peeking through the curtain, I saw that no other office lights were on. I paced near the door. The previous job of Juilliard's current president had been at a real school. An *Ivy League* school. Surely this was behavior he would frown upon. My anxiety meter ran from high to higher: what the fuck was I doing here?

Dennis picked up the test from Mr. Moss's desk and called me over to look at it. My back was to the door when a key turned in the lock, and for a moment it felt as though the tiny office had turned into a concert hall holding 3,000 hushed souls, and I was alone onstage, listening to the blood rush to my head as my heart tried to engineer a stroke.

A woman came in. "Hi," she said, shyly.

"Hi!" said Dennis.

She asked us to excuse her as she picked up Mr. Moss's wastebasket. She took it to the hallway and emptied it into her cart.

"No problem," Dennis said.

We took the test back down the long hallway to the library, made a copy, then returned it to Mr. Moss's office.

I dutifully memorized all of the answers, though by the time Mr. Moss returned the tests, the facts were forgotten. Due to the addition of a bonus question, I got 105 percent.

If I had cheated at a real school, I would be forced to consider that this was not my finest moment. At Juilliard, I thought I should be commended for my initiative. If classes and tests were a part of attending Juilliard, I would make the effort. If making the effort meant giving up practice time, I would cheat.

⁊

Exams mattered not a bit to us; performances were how we measured our progress through Juilliard. You could not cheat your way through practicing, because once you were up on that stage, utterly exposed, how well and how much you'd practiced would be evident to all the coughing, paper-rustling, throat-clearing souls in the audience.

Caroline and I had decided to play Bartok's Sonata for Two Pianos and Percussion. We'd had four months to rehearse, something we would never have in the real world. We might get hired to play the Bartok again, if and when we became professionals. But then we'd be paid to rehearse. There would be four professional schedules to work around, four people with obligations to fulfill. Without a school to rehearse in, space for two pianos and all our percussion instruments would be hard to find. We had the chance to play this piece better now than we would ever play it again.

Technically at least, Caroline and I now had our names on Broadway. On the sidewalk Juilliard shared with Alice Tully Hall were huge glass-encased posters. In the urban forest, these were the trees. If you walked along this angled stretch of Broadway, you could find out what was happening in Alice Tully on a given night.

Our given night was January 16, 1987. We'd had our

dress rehearsal that morning, and now Caroline and I were trying to get through the day. We were utterly rudderless. The only compensation for having a day filled with so much pressure was the guilt-free breaking of all the rules. There was no routine. Other than warming up, we didn't practice. No listening to music, no need to decide whether or not to skip a class. Both sets of our parents had come to town for the performance and we had to make the effort to greet and then ignore them.

My mom had brought us an apple pie. We filled some of the afternoon hours sitting on the floor of my apartment eating it. We dug in with two forks, stabbing at whatever section we felt like, for me the brown sugar and butter crumble, for Caroline the barely sweetened crust. Like an old couple, we argued about desserts; Caroline was always trying to understand my criteria for calling something dessert — why an item had to have chocolate, why oatmeal cookies were basically bread. I, who ate frosting out of a can, was always trying to understand her indifference to sugar. I accused her of goading me; I would never accept that she wasn't abstaining just to show off her willpower.

Finally the sun went down, and even though we had three more hours to fill, it was now the evening of our concert. We dressed in our concert black, warmed up, went onstage to set up and then recheck our setups. Our pianists showed up and warmed up onstage.

By seven o'clock, the backstage area was beginning to get crowded. The stage manager and stagehands were there; students playing in the other groups were arriving. I picked up my knapsack and headed toward the bathroom. I felt secretive, furtive, although there was no reason for anyone to bother wondering about what I was doing. If a fellow musician had nothing better to do, she could imagine me pulling tampons out of the knapsack and being greatly pissed off that this huge concert couldn't fall on a day that didn't include bleeding as a distraction.

I passed through the dressing room with its lockers and ratty couch, went into the empty bathroom, and locked myself into a stall. I checked my watch. It was 7:05, exactly the right time. From my knapsack I took out my tiny plastic container of Inderal and removed the cotton ball inside. The cotton kept the pills from becoming dust as they bounced around in my knapsack. I put five of the pills under my tongue. This was 100 milligrams of Inderal — the most I'd ever taken all at once and two and a half times the amount the doctor had recommended. From the Met audition, I'd learned that I would need this much. I flushed the toilet, for form's sake, and went to the drinking fountain in the hall. By the time I had maneuvered the pills around in my mouth and swallowed them, they had left spots of unfeeling on the underside of my tongue.

Now I had an hour to fill. The aspect of performing that was the hardest on my nerves was that it had to happen not when *I* was ready, but when the audience had filled the theater. We might be able to choose the exact moment we started the piece, but once we started that was it. Didn't matter if I had an itch or had to cough or if my head was ready to explode and spray blood across the stage, I had to play *right now*. And the Bartok was a much-loved percussion standard. For those familiar with the piece, listening to us play it would be an experience similar to that of an art lover walking into a museum to gaze at Picasso's *Guernica*. They would expect the work of art to look exactly as they had remembered.

There was so much time involved in the "before" — the practicing, rehearsing, anticipation, excitement, self-doubt — and then the "after" — the drinking, evaluating, congratulating, reliving. The piece itself was only 25 minutes long and, during that time, while disaster waited politely in the wings, there was finally more action than thought. We played and then it was over, and there wasn't a thing in the performance we would have done differently.

I'd never had that happen before. All four of us felt the same way — we were ecstatic. Now we let ourselves think about who was in the audience. It was like telling a ghost story in the safety of daylight — we thrilled each other with who we'd seen, who among our teachers and former teachers had come to hear us. Now we could be glad we'd given Richard a Walkman to tape it for us.

~

Richard came to many of our performances, sometimes with his wife, sometimes alone. We were always playing for him. No one else in the audience knew better how we measured up, no one else knew our strengths and weaknesses like Richard. I was comfortable with him there; with one of us onstage and one in the audience, our relationship made sense.

He came to another of our performances that spring, a concert in Avery Fisher Hall. Fisher, neighbor to Juilliard and home of the New York Philharmonic, was a strange place to play — it appeared that the architects had been more concerned with their vision of concert hall as boxy rectangle than they were with concertgoer comfort. How else to explain that if you were seated on one of the upper floors and facing forward in your chair, you would be looking not at the stage, but at your fellow patrons on the other side of the hall?

But to be standing on that stage was thrilling. To look out and see the ground-floor seats filling up, to see the squirming patrons on the sides as they tried to turn and face the stage — that was exciting. We were playing a huge, ambitious classic — Bartok's Concerto for Orchestra. Just like he did with his sonata, Bartok began the second movement with solo snare drum. And, as with our sonata performance earlier in the year, I would be the one playing it.

And fuck if I wasn't as tightly wound as one of those coiled trick snakes in a can.

We'd already finished the first half of the concert, and now, during the intermission, I was wandering around backstage. I walked down the half flight of stairs to one of the musician warm-up areas, fingering the 40 milligrams of Inderal in the pocket of my black pants. There was an empty chair in the corner, and I sat there with a program, pretending to read the bios. In fact, I was calculating. At seven I'd taken 60 milligrams of Inderal, which had peaked at their maximum potency at eight, just as we were beginning the concert. Now it was nine o'clock, what would be the actual amount still in my bloodstream? And how long was the first movement of the Bartok? The stage manager called 15 minutes left in the intermission. So I now had 15 minutes plus the first movement until my solo. If Inderal took an hour to be at its most effective, how much should I take right now in order to still have some working a half hour from now?

It seemed to make sense to err on the side of taking too much. As I headed up the stairs, my back was to the musicians in the room. I pinched the pills, brought them to my mouth and made like I was picking my teeth. By the time I'd reached the top of the stairs, the pills were under my tongue. To the musicians backstage, I was just getting a drink at the fountain.

The second half began and there was nothing to do during the first movement except obsess. Caroline and Sebastian were with me in the back row. What if I'd taken too much? I could be sitting between them, listening to the first movement and suddenly pitch forward in a dead faint. The resonant sound of my body hitting the stage would stop the show. Caroline and Sebastian would meet the ambulance at St. Luke's–Roosevelt. *She overdosed*, he'd say. My secret would be out.

Inderal and I had enjoyed a two-year honeymoon during which time I could play anything with confidence. Now I had this new problem — the fear of shaking had been replaced by the fear of not getting the dosage correct. I had to balance the amount of Inderal with the amount of performance anxiety, a very personal and inexact science. A balance between shaking and passing out, shaking and Karen Ann Quinlan, shaking and death. There was no formula for which I could plug in Bartok Concerto for Orchestra/solo snare drum/Avery Fisher Hall and have it spit out the correct number of pills. I didn't know what was too much because there seemed to be no one I could, or would, ask.

So now I fidgeted, waiting for the second movement, wiggling my toes fiercely, trying to keep the blood moving back to my heart. I crossed my legs one way, uncrossed them, crossed them the other way. I looked at my hands, folded and resting in my lap. What did the audience see? Certainly I looked calm and professional. Thinking about the audience reminded me of something Donald had mentioned during a timpani lesson. In a recent concert someone in the audience had stood up and screamed, "Fuck you!" The patron had then followed that with (and here, Donald's voice became a whisper) "Fuck God!" Ushers escorted him out. The orchestra kept playing. What if I decided to scream? Was it a decision or did it just burst out of you when it was most inappropriate? Would I, too, say, "Fuck God," because now I could not get that phrase out of my head, or would I come up with something worse? What was worse than "Fuck God"? I wondered if Inderal helped with impulse control.

We were nearing the end of the first movement. I knew that thinking about *not* making a mistake while playing made me imagine the mistake in my head, which actually increased the likelihood I would make it. Then I had to consciously *not* think about not thinking about making a mistake, which made me think I was going to vomit. That, at least, gave me something else to think about.

At the end of the first movement, I slowly stood up and picked up my sticks. The audience coughed, shifted in their seats. The winds swabbed their instruments, the brass players blew out spit. When the conductor raised his baton, there was a moment of church silence. He locked eyes with me, gave me an upbeat, and I played.

Nerves of Inderal.

≀

After my next lesson, Richard and I sat at the diner and talked about the concert. He praised the solo. I had done it exactly right, he said, especially the diminuendo at the end. I squirmed — the only thing hard about playing softly at the end of the second movement was doing it while your hands shook. I had cheated.

It was an easier dinner than usual; I was always happy to have a focus to our discussion. We talked about the concert, and I stretched the topic as far as I could. I barely let him answer one question before I asked another. When we finished our sandwiches, the waitress appeared and took our dishes away, balancing them on one forearm.

When she was gone, Richard reached for my hands. I put them on the table, and they were so stiff with tension they felt almost electrified.

He held my hands gently and stroked them, but instead of staring into my eyes and smiling, he started talking about the rest of the Bartok. The expression on his face was serious. There were things I very much needed to improve, he said. I could play soft dynamics, but when I really needed to stand out I tended to fade into the texture of the orchestra. I had to add spark — that little bit of speed before the end of a crescendo, accents that jumped out at you, carrying the musical phrase to its logical conclusion. I was looking at him earnestly, taking it in, trying like the good student that I was to understand.

"Caroline put it well," he said. "She said, 'Patti is a light player.'"

Richard had finally said something that broke my stone face. I started to cry.

He looked surprised. "That really hits you where you live," he said cheerfully.

Caroline's opinion of me mattered as much as Richard's. She didn't say I was a great player who had trouble playing loudly; she labeled me a "light" player. It sounded like Caroline didn't think I was going to be able to overcome that.

"You see, Caroline has 'it,'" Richard said. He shook a fist in the air to define "it." He reached his other hand out for mine and, when I refused, he laughed, like I was just being a sulky teenager. "The guy that was standing next to you has 'it,' too," he said. "Now we just need to work on *you*."

It took me a minute; I had to think about the stage. The "guy" he was referring to was Sebastian. Richard wasn't saying Sebastian's name now.

He'd just told me Caroline had doubts about me as a player; he wouldn't refer to Sebastian by name. I didn't know which stunned me more. Caroline's pronouncement made me feel overwhelmed. I was already exhausted by how much I needed to learn.

But practicing and improving, as least, were always under my control, while Richard's opinion of Sebastian was not. Had something happened between them? The real feeling of dread came from this: did it have to do with me?

As we walked back to school, Richard kept his hand on my back, steering me across Columbus and Broadway as if I were fragile. I was usually careful to slow my pace for him, but now, chafing at the hand on my back, I didn't bother.

"Slow down for the old man," he said.

Richard followed me to my locker. He was on my right, and when I swung open the door, I didn't care that it was between us. He walked around it, grinning. My mind was on practicing now, and I felt better just thinking about it. Looking into my locker, I gathered my sticks, some music, and my snare drum. Aware, suddenly, that I was being petulant and that Richard was enjoying it, I took care not to slam the locker door. The percussion hall was quiet, no one in the hallway, no sounds coming from the studios. Complete silence was so uncommon in a music school, I felt like I was about to be the victim of a surprise party.

While I set up in Richard's studio, he went on again about this extra dimension my playing needed, the added excitement. Not to worry, he explained, it was something that could be fixed. We would work on it.

"It's my job to teach you," he said. He stood next to me, looking benign and comical, his trench coat still buttoned up around his big stomach, his hand clutching his black bag. He made no move to leave. He was still grinning. I adjusted my snare-drum stand and got out my metronome and music. Finally, he set his bag down on the floor and reached over for a hug.

Hugging Richard wasn't uncomfortable, it felt not at all like holding his hand did, it was just affectionate and normal. Of course, the reason it felt normal was because he also hugged Caroline and Sharon. I was so glad he was leaving, I put my sticks on the stand and reached around his wide chest. When I went to pull back, he stopped me. His hands moved from my back to my upper arms, and gripped. Then he kissed me. I froze.

Frowning, he pulled back. "Someone needs to teach you how to kiss," he said.

He leaned in again. Because my eyes were open, I could see that his were closed, and this time he moved his lips around, pushing against mine. I was frozen, my arms at my sides, my eyes fixed on the door. When he pulled away, there was no sound. He picked up his black bag, gave me a cheerful wave, and left me alone.

14
Tribal Breakup

As graduation quietly crept closer, the tribe began to unravel. We were spending too much time together. Issues that should've been little became big. Everybody was mad at everybody else. I was mad at no one until I became mad at everyone for being mad at each other. I was trying to ignore my panic about Richard, his feelings for me, his having kissed me. Then Sebastian and I broke up and it got worse.

We hadn't been the kind of couple who were going to last. I didn't pretend we could win the lottery twice and get jobs in the same city. There was one couple at Juilliard whom I was fascinated by — Diane, a bassoonist, and Jerry, a bass player. They'd actually gotten married in their last year at school. I didn't understand: why go to Juilliard if getting a job wasn't your passion? How could they think that getting married made sense when they didn't know where — if they were lucky — they would get jobs? As it happened, Jerry got a job in the Cincinnati Symphony. I imagined their lives in fast-forward — Diane gamely begins her freelance career in Cincinnati (telling herself it's only temporary), driving many miles to Columbus or even Kentucky for work, and when she's lucky, she's asked to sub with Jerry's orchestra. She continues to take auditions: they worry about what to do if she actually wins an audition, when she actually wins an audition. Jerry settles into his rewarding job: concerts, big paychecks, tours. Then a bassoon position opens up in the Cincinnati Symphony. Their non-musician friends, people like their neighbors who are clueless about the odds, say, *Isn't that great?* Diane practices constantly but she doesn't get the job, doesn't even get out of the preliminary round. They have a baby and still she practices. Then they have another and another, and she stops practicing because there isn't time. At this point she is primarily a mom and also a little bit addicted to Valium, which keeps her from asking herself whether or not she'd have gotten a job if she'd waited to get married.

For Sebastian and me, it had just been too much to ask: to share a teacher and colleagues and practice space and a goal; to compete for parts in orchestra, for summer festivals, and for attention. Eventually, we would be at the same auditions competing for the same jobs. It was impossible to forget how limited were the resources for which we were competing. It was exhausting. We had been wading in the same small pool, and one of us had to get out. Our greatest strength had been our friendship and there would be a break before we could return to that. It was such a loss. We spent most of our time alone, but without the connection between us, that time was lonelier.

꒰

It had been a month since Richard had kissed me in his studio. That night, he had left and I had picked up my sticks and started practicing. Since the beginning of the school year, I'd been great at not thinking. But it was all still there, this great unarticulated mess, festering. Occasionally, in the middle of practicing and not thinking, I would be struck by a thought anyway: *This "situation" now includes physical contact.* Before he kissed me, I could easily dismiss the problem — *He's just saying things. He's not doing anything.* Now things had changed. Instead of thinking about his behavior, I thought about mine. Why had he kissed me? Wasn't I supposed to say, *Don't do that?* Had I done anything to invite it?

It was the same kind of queasy I got from walking by a group of construction workers. I'd be on the sidewalk and think, *I'm the only one here, I'm a girl, they're all guys,* and I'd feel some anxiety and dread because I didn't know how to act — eyes down? Stare straight ahead? Tight smile? The real conflict comes from this: that stroll is a lose-lose situation. Feel bad if they whistle and bad if they don't. Objectified or ignored.

This was the part I couldn't resolve. We *wanted* attention from Richard. We sought his approval. By not behaving differently, did I make him think *this* kind of attention was okay? I felt now like I was walking a very narrow line. On one side was more unwanted attention; on the other was getting dumped by Richard for not accepting that attention.

Don't think.

Since our talk after the Avery Fisher concert, Richard had been very serious about helping me to develop "it." Throughout April and into May, he'd come to my lessons armed with exercises he'd created. I needed to add drama to my playing, but I needed the technique to pull off that drama. None of it came naturally to me; I was playing it safe, but I didn't know how to change. Richard broke it down with suggestions like this: *Delay the crescendo until the last minute and then speed up the roll.* That I could do.

{

Caroline and I decided to play the Bartok sonata again for our year-end jury. This jury would also unceremoniously serve as my audition for the master's program. We set up in room 309, the only space big enough for two grand pianos, four timpani, a xylophone, a bass drum, snare drums, cymbals, and our audience of two — Richard and the timpani teacher, Donald — whom we'd seated at a table in the front and only row.

It was less exciting our second time but also easier, which for me, was now measured by the amount of Inderal taken. Instead of the 100 milligrams I'd taken for the concert, I took only 60. When we finished 25 minutes later, I looked up from the snare drum to see Richard stumbling toward me, arms outstretched, crying. I wondered what the pianists and Donald thought of this reaction. There was a section in the first movement that had some fast crescendo rolls on snare drum, one that required the very "it" we'd been working on, and from his reaction I guessed I had proven I could add drama to my playing. Or at least I'd improved. Or maybe I'd just done it this one time.

With my jury behind me, with "it" conquered, with the completion of one useless degree approaching, there was little to focus on apart from my sadness over the breakup with Sebastian. I was too tired to hide it and made the colossal mistake of allowing Richard to notice. I had never told Richard anything about my personal life — never told him Sebastian and I were a couple nor that we'd broken up. At school, we'd only looked and acted like friends. In my last lesson of the year, after he'd repeatedly asked what was wrong, I finally told him I'd had a falling-out with a friend.

The next day he cornered me in Donald's room. I was practicing xylophone, waiting for a rehearsal to start in room 309. I heard the door open, but assumed it was just another student looking for something. By the time I glanced up, Richard was standing in front of me.

He wasn't smiling. He didn't say hello. He just picked up a stool and set it at the end of the xylophone. My heart couldn't pound — because of the rehearsal coming up, I had taken Inderal an hour before — but I felt my face flush. Apparently that was still possible. As Richard arranged himself on the stool, resting his hands on his knees to hold back the momentum of his upper body, I saw that his forehead was furrowed and the lines continued all the way back to his former hairline. He looked old.

There was no warm-up to his question. "I've been thinking about what you told me," he said. "Was it Sebastian?"

"Yes."

He asked what happened.

"It was a falling-out," I said.

"About what?"

I had to get out. "I have rehearsal," I said. I took my music off the stand and laid it flat on the xylophone. Richard was sitting at the lower end, and as I was about to push, he braced himself on the frame.

"What was the falling-out about?"

"I have to go," I said. I was pleading. Now we could hear the hall filling up with musicians. Noise in the hall meant that break had started and I needed to load the xylophone in before it was over. I pulled the xylophone toward me so that Richard had to let go; I pushed it around him, and wheeled it into the hall. This rehearsal was for a Juilliard tour to Asia. In just three days I would get to leave school, and when we returned two and a half weeks later, it would officially be summer and Richard would have no reason to be there.

{

I tried to avoid school. A few weeks earlier, looking ahead to the empty days that would follow the tour, I had decided I needed a job. A regular job, the kind that was okay for now, but one I would be horrified to discover myself doing after I finished with Juilliard. I found one at a kids' clothing store on Columbus Avenue. It would give me a few hours a week of scheduled time and serve the same mind-clearing purpose that classes did during the year.

Two days before we left for the tour, after a day spent folding clothes and asking customers if I could help them find a particular size, I walked from the air-conditioned store onto the steamy sidewalk and saw Richard. He came toward me in kind of a crouch and I realized he'd been leaning against a fire hydrant. My face fell.

I turned uptown to walk the two blocks to my apartment. Richard walked beside me. When I turned to cross Columbus, we were facing each other. I wanted him to leave before I crossed the street; I didn't want him to follow me to my apartment.

"Are you in love with Sebastian?" he asked.

"I love all my friends," I said. I was pleading.

Richard left.

The next day was Sunday, and I was home packing for the tour. All our instruments would be going in cargo crates, so I only needed to pack sticks and clothes. My phone rang and it was Richard. He wanted to know, he said, how Sebastian and I had been involved.

I was sitting at my desk, something I never did. Why would I? To do homework? Write a letter? The desk had been there when I moved in. I looked around my apartment, my tiny sanctuary. I could easily lie on the floor and touch one wall with my feet, and with my hands over my head touch the other. Its length from door to window was less than two cars.

Richard was waiting for me to say something.

Sebastian didn't deserve whatever punishment Richard wanted to serve him just because he'd been dating me. I said I had to go and hung up.

I called Caroline. We'd never talked about Richard and I didn't elaborate now; I said only that Richard was "in a bad way." I asked if she would call him and see that he was okay. She asked no questions and said she would.

I unplugged the phone and turned on the radio. I listened to news all the time now; it was background static that replaced any thoughts that came into my head. "You give us 22 minutes; we'll give you the world," they promised, and sure enough, about three times an hour I could hear the headlines, the weather, the status of traffic as it existed on all those acronymic roads: the BQE, the LIE, the GW Bridge. If I listened long enough, the news would slowly change. Accidents were cleared away, it rained and then it stopped raining, and eventually all conflicts were resolved.

The tour. For months afterward, Caroline refused to speak its name — she wouldn't say "tour" and eventually she stopped using her own abbreviation of "T." If she had to refer to those 16 days, three countries, and eight concerts, she called it "that word."

For most of the orchestra, since we didn't live together in dorms, this was like a frat party. It started on the plane — for 12 hours from New York, through the vast whiteness of Canada, up and over Alaska, to Tokyo. The orchestra drank and ate, switched seats, and mingled like it was a flying cocktail party. There was time to get drunk, have a hangover, and get drunk again. That part was fun. Spending so much time together with Sebastian without being together was painful.

The orchestra as a whole was wildly incurious about the countries we were about to tour. We were going to places so foreign to our bodies that we had to get gamma globulin shots, yet I wasn't aware of anyone making an effort to learn about these countries beforehand. I didn't even see any copies of *Fodor's China* being passed around. Our attitude wasn't indifference — the per diem, the four-star hotels, invitation by actual communists — this was what the big orchestras did and it was exciting. But it was also work. We were playing huge, demanding programs: Stravinsky's *Rite of Spring*, *Medea's Meditation and Dance of Vengeance* by Samuel Barber, Beethoven's Third Symphony, Bartok's Second Violin Concerto. These pieces were hard to play under the best of circumstances. We had to be able to play them jet-lagged and without the usual amount of practice time.

At our first stop, we found ourselves in a country

whose citizens prized order and rules and schedules. We big Americans set out from the Akasaka Prince Hotel and were amazed when a crowd of people, all with the same hair color, stood patiently on a street corner waiting for the light to change, though there wasn't a car in sight. We also learned from our tour manager, that *yes* in Japanese might mean *yes* or *yes* might mean *no*.

The hardest piece I had to play on the tour was *Medea*, which started with an exposed xylophone solo. It might have been interesting to know the story of Medea, to really understand it — did I, playing the xylophone, represent the hag with the snakes in her hair? But at a concert or audition, nobody cared if we could explain the piece. I would have *said* it mattered; I would have made a case, if pressed, that being able to visualize Medea's head covered in snakes helped me to phrase the opening solo in a pointy, tongue-darting kind of way. But if I went to an audition knowing the story, fully able to analyze Medea's relationship to other she-monsters of the ancient world, and then played like crap, that time spent in the library would have been worse than useless, it would have been time I should've been practicing. And even if that studying had led me to realize the character I was actually visualizing all that time was *Medusa*, it wouldn't have made a bit of difference. During the tour, it was far more important that I get to the hall early and try to find some practice time on the xylophone.

We played three concerts in Japan with their home-grown teenage violin star, Midori, as soloist, and after the final one we packed up our cases. Our job was just to get all the instruments into these travel trunks; a crew was responsible for loading them onto trucks and airplanes. On the bus to the airport, we were given a stern lecture. If we were so stupid as to have brought drugs this far, it was time to dump them. We were headed to a country whose officials couldn't possibly know that a certain bass player would sooner sell his bass to its citizens than sell his pot. Neither would they care.

The next morning we left for China. Our first stop was Beijing. We were staying at what was, in 1987, one of their best hotels, a wide white building of four or five stories set against a lush green hillside. I didn't catch the name, Blossom Something or Palace Something. Maybe Blossom Palace. Inside, the lobby was tiled in blue and white, from floors to walls, like a bathroom.

The hotel was responsible for our first breakfast. For two years now, ever since barfing Hairy's undercooked meatloaf in Colorado, I'd been a vegetarian. I had visions of Chinese food in China being just like Empire Szechuan on Columbus Avenue — stir-fried vegetables, sesame noodles, egg drop soup. We sat down in the main dining room and a group of women in aprons circled the tables, pouring tea. They were unsmiling. They disappeared into the kitchen, then returned, each carrying four plates. Solemnly, they presented our meal, an omelet. One each, a plain half-moon of eggs with three or four peas inside.

Very quickly, in five or six bites, there was rumbling within the orchestra. A whispered conference broke out between our tour coordinator and the women. They understood the word *more* but not the concept, just as we didn't understand *limited supply*. They had no more food to give us.

Hungry, we loaded the buses for a day of sightseeing. We bumped along a dirt road, spewing exhaust on the bikers we passed. They were ferrying huge loads of hay, these bikes. At an intersection of dirt roads, our driver pulled the bus over and got out. He left us idling and fuming and disappeared into a wooden hut. We appeared to be in a town square. Outside of my window was a bulletin board standing on two stick legs. It was covered with pictures. Before we started moving again, I focused on an image of a young man, looking quite dead. He lay on his back, naked from the waist up and bloody, with cuts on his chest and face.

We bounced along, keeping pace with the bicycles until we came to the wall that was our destination. Up close, the Great Wall was not the beautiful and lush green that it was in pictures. In those gorgeous *National Geographic* photos taken from high above, the area looked like a forest with a stately wall winding through it. I was surprised how much greenery was growing between the stones, but the land all around the wall was brown. From the ground it was hard to be impressed by the wall's size — the structures I saw every day were vertical. Lay the World Trade Center towers on their sides, and they wouldn't look so monumental either.

The fun was on the wall itself. We were left to explore on our own, told to return to the buses at a certain time. Caroline and I set off together and soon discovered we were walking behind "Barbie," our president's wife. She was young and beautiful and had nothing to do on the trip except change from well-coordinated day ensembles into fancier night ones. Thus, Barbie. The Chinese had thought of almost everything — gun turrets, guards' towers, retractable ladders. They just hadn't imagined heels. We walked behind Barbie and watched her carefully pick her way along the irregular stones.

Our third stop on the tour was Shanghai. When we arrived, we discovered we'd been bumped from our hotel

— our reservations had been changed to a lesser hotel to make way for some steroidal women's sports team. It was here that Barbie found her purpose and her voice and set about pitching an interpreted fit. She and her Ken, outraged on our behalf, stood in the lobby and negotiated with the tour guides to find a better hotel for us.

What Barbie didn't realize: we *lived* in hotels worse than this. While they ranted, we picked up our keys and found our rooms.

After we'd settled in, Caroline and I went to the hotel's bar. It was already filled with students. We were at the midpoint of the tour, and because it was a big travel day we had the rest of the evening off. Most of the orchestra was here and it was odd to see this group of people in the same room but without instruments. The whole orchestra, just drinking and talking. We recounted the last concert, how Joe, one of the horn players, had gotten sick during *Rite of Spring*. Not to be undone by a little food poisoning, he turned around in his chair, puked off the back of the riser, then finished the piece.

Caroline, Gary, and I decided to go looking for a music store that could sell us some real Chinese instruments. We got enough information from the tour guide to have a taxi take us to a percussion shop.

While our music stores back home were big and loud, this shop was just a tiny storefront in an alley. It was quiet. No brats banging on drum sets. No showroom at all. Just two glass cases of instruments — authentic Chinese instruments. That was why we were excited. There were temple blocks, wood blocks, cymbals, and gongs. We pointed, and the clerk retrieved. Between the three of us, we were spending a great deal of yuan. The clerk was quiet as he shuffled around for us, getting drums from the back. We were used to a quickening hustle and the big smile of capitalistic commissioned glee. This man could sell a lot of stuff or not sell a lot of stuff; either way he'd finish work and get paid the same and go home to the cinder-block apartment he shared with his wife and kids and parents.

A crowd had gathered at the door. They watched us try out cymbals and tom-toms. And when we finally left, we were hauling tom-toms, cymbals, gongs, and bags of wood blocks and temple blocks.

Our concerts in China had been wildly successful. We were the first American conservatory orchestra to tour there. Now that I'd gotten real Chinese instruments from China, there was nothing else I wanted from this tour. At an outdoor party given by our hosts in the city of Guangzhou, the buffet was plentiful and good. Full for the first time in two weeks, I lay on the grass and looked at the stars and realized they were the same stars that hovered unseen above the Manhattan skyline.

We took a train from Guangzhou to Hong Kong. There, except for the writing on the signs, it felt like we were getting closer to home. It was dirty — not in a fecal way like China, but in a modern, urban way, with graffiti and trash and soot. There was fast food to be eaten and stuff to be purchased. We could do that in New York. It was time to go home.

15
Summer

Just before we left for the tour, Juilliard's 1987 graduation ceremony had taken place. I hadn't gone. Graduating from Juilliard was not to be confused with an actual accomplishment. What could we celebrate? That another hundred or so musicians, actors, and dancers had leapt from the diving board into the great and swirling pit of the unemployed? I had skipped classes and cheated on tests. The only worthy thing I'd done while at school was practice, and the only graduation from that would be to get a job. I didn't even bother to pick up the piece of paper that proclaimed me, appropriately enough, a BM.

I spent the day of my graduation folding and selling clothes with my coworker Jeremy. I couldn't ignore the fact that four years had gone by, and — unless I won an audition — I would soon be unemployed. He understood — he had just graduated from the Fashion Institute of Technology. That he'd once worn one green and one blue contact lens was more relevant to his future career in fashion than was his diploma.

When I first moved to New York, I had seen what an ex-Juilliard student looked like. Among the index cards in the housing file was one from a girl who had graduated three months earlier and wanted a roommate to share her apartment. My dad and I had gone to see her one-bedroom at the Milburn Hotel on 76th and Broadway.

The girl greeted us at the door. She invited us in and the three of us stood wedged in the foyer while she explained that there was a third roommate, a person with a "real" job. She turned and opened the foyer's closet door. Just like in Willy Wonka's factory, there was another smaller door at the rear. They'd taken down the back wall so that when the regular person came home from her regular job, she wouldn't have to disturb her two roommates by walking through the living room.

The girl led us out of the foyer and into the main room. A row of bookshelves, about chest-high, divided the room in two. On her side was a neatly made bed with her horn resting on top, as well as a dresser, a desk, and a stereo. Her Juilliard bachelor of music degree was framed and hung above her bed. The other side of the room had a wavy wooden floor and was empty.

I looked at her, this girl whose name was Susan; I looked at her horn, which she'd obviously been practicing before we'd shown up. It seemed to me she was gamely sticking to a schedule. While she was a student, she'd structured her days around practicing; now she would still structure her days around practicing. But now she was "trying to get the freelance thing going" and "taking auditions" and she'd lost her full-time identity as a student, as one of the hopeful. As she stood on her side of the room, and I stood across the room on the bare sloping floor, the only thing between us was four years.

Susan would have to decide how long she would be able to keep trying. She would either get a job or make the decision to give up. I couldn't live with her.

≀

I was going to spend one more year at school. Juilliard's requirements were so negligible that for those of us who'd already done four years, it was easy to do a fifth and come away with two degrees. There was no oral exam or thesis or recital involved in becoming a master of music. My last jury had counted as my official audition for the master's program, so without any real formality I would start working on a new degree that mattered as little as the first. But I would have lessons and a place to practice for one more year. I was aware that if I finished that degree and still had not won an audition, I would need to add some concrete details to my vague plan of "continuing to improve." Details such as where to live, where to practice, and how to earn money.

≀

Even though I should have gotten myself into Tanglewood (I'd been wait-listed again), I was happy being in New York. Summer was the best time of year in Manhattan and it belonged to those of us who stayed. It was humid, the garbage stank, slime ran in the gutters, and the rich fled. What they didn't realize was how much room they made for the rest of us. Late on Friday afternoons, on the Upper East Side and on Central Park West, the rich idled their Volvos in front of their buildings while the door-men loaded them with dogs and gear, then they began their clogged race toward the exits from Manhattan. Destinations: Long Island, Connecticut, the Jersey Shore.

Once they were gone and traffic was lighter, Manhattan smelled different. Almost fresh. The sidewalks were less crowded. While the part-timers swam in the ocean, we lounged on our grass beach. In this city of concrete, the Sheep Meadow was cherished grass, the crown jewel within the crown jewel of Central Park. Fenced off from the rest of the park, it looked like a carpet of grass, like a suburban lawn in one of those movie-set neighborhoods where the mansions look perfect and identical. The fence was locked from November to April, when thousands of feet would have turned it to mud. All of this protection so that for the few months of summer we could feel the waxy grass between our bare toes, lather up with lotion, and lay on our towels, looking up at the buildings of the midtown skyline above the trees.

It was a relief to go to school now and know that Caroline and I were the only two drummers there. No one else was in our hall, and no one came into the studios. We showed up at eight a.m. and each had a practice room for as long as we wanted. Some days the only other person I'd see would be Wayne. He was a bassoon player, fulfilling his work-study job by cutting out torn sections of the orange wallpaper in the hallway and replacing them with patches. He was back in school after a reputed suspension following his conduct in a performance of Strauss's *Also Sprach Zarathustra*. Better known as the theme from the movie *2001: A Space Odyssey*, *Zarathustra* begins with a long low note held by basses, organ, and contrabassoon. For some reason, the conductor decided he didn't want contra and told Wayne to leave the note out. There was no arguing this point. An orchestra is a dictatorship and the conductor a dictator. Wayne complied. For the rehearsals.

There was this concept at school called "taking it out at the concert." I remembered being floored at the first concert I played at Juilliard. We rehearsed Rachmaninoff's *Symphonic Dances*, with a drummer named Jim playing timpani. In rehearsals all week, he played loudly or softly, following the music's dictates with appropriate dynamics. Then at the concert Jim came in with the first entrance of the piece and played three times louder than he'd ever played it at any rehearsal.

Like Jim, Wayne took it out at the concert. The conductor gave the downbeat, and along with the basses and the organ came the flapping raspberry sound of the contrabassoon. It was like a low-flying plane was buzzing the orchestra. The conductor *stopped* the concert, waved Wayne out, and began again. Wayne had been "fired." He was famous for it.

Now he was back doing pointless work replacing these wallpaper scraps. Come September, we'd wheel our unwieldy percussion carts down the hall and scrape off the new pieces.

꒰

After a few weeks of this solitude, we started preparing for a concert. Ethan Shipper, the contemporary ensemble conductor at school, had started a new concert series at the Museum of Modern Art and he'd asked us to put together an evening of percussion ensemble music.

The centerpiece of the concert was *Third Construction*, a quartet by the composer John Cage. If the Bartok sonata had become a classic by expanding how conventional percussion instruments could be incorporated into a piece of chamber music and taught to "behave" well enough to play alongside a pair of pianos, Cage threw all of that out the window and introduced the percussion ensemble as a group capable of combining standard instruments with sounds from the junkyard.

For this composition, each player needed five tin cans. We nailed together pieces of wood for frames and strung paint cans between them. We "tuned" the cans — that is, we made five different pitches by taking sticks and smacking the crap out of each in turn. This was the piece we'd been thinking of when we bought those Chinese tom-toms. We each needed three, and instead of renting, like most drummers had to, we got to use our own.

Third Construction featured a "lion's roar" at one point. This was made by tying off a long length of string and passing it through a hole made in the head of a drum. The string rested on its knot; when you pinched it and gently pulled, it caused the head of the drum to vibrate. It *roared*.

About three-quarters of the way into the piece came the introduction of the conch shell. It was the same huge shell with pink and white swirls you could find on a beach in Florida, had the tourist vendors not collected them all to sell. Caroline sanded the pointed end smooth and played it like a trumpet. By moving one hand in and out of the shell's aperture, she could raise and lower the pitch.

Sebastian and Rick came back to town to join Caroline and me. After a week spent rehearsing in Donald's studio, we felt we were ready for an audience and asked Ethan to come and listen to us.

Here it was, the height of summer in an airless room, and Ethan arrived in his khaki pants and long-sleeved white shirt. Didn't he have a summer version of this uniform? I tried to imagine him in shorts. He made his way around the room, tapping on the tin cans, trying the lion's roar, smiling and showing his crooked teeth. He loved percussion. We sat him at the head of the group, where he crossed his legs and rested his hands in his lap. He looked bizarrely casual.

The piece starts softly. Rick began with a solo for three tom-toms, playing with his fingers instead of sticks. We played for less than a minute before Ethan stopped us.

"You *could* play it that way," he said. He sounded like he wanted to follow that with *if you wanted to be musically lazy and interpret the entire piece incorrectly.*

He told us that Cage used bar lines — the lines that clump groups of notes into a measure — as a convenience. They were not to be regarded as measures of 4/4 in the conventional sense, where the emphasis is on beats one and three. The lines should be accented and phrased according to the grouping of notes Cage had fashioned, many of which disregarded the presence of the bar line entirely.

Oh.

Ethan explained this patiently, but there was a weariness about him; he'd given speeches like this before. His was a world where very few were as bright as he. I imagined that in every interaction, musical or otherwise, he always hoped to come across an intellectual equal and yet expected to be disappointed.

In that expectation we didn't disappoint him. We had assumed he was just going to be a warm body to play for, a dress-rehearsal audience of one who would listen to the whole piece, then praise our hard work and enthusiasm. Since we could not incorporate a complete paradigm shift in a day, we cheated. We added accents to the beginnings of groupings and resisted the instinct to add them artificially at the bar line.

On Friday night at the Modern Museum of Art we could have played it either way — the audience's reaction would've been the same. They screamed. They loved it. They were already congratulating themselves for attending a *modern* music concert. Add to that the drinks, the light in the sculpture garden dimming slowly over the course of the concert, the Picasso goat with his belly nearly touching the ground. Add to that the big-bang ending of the *Third Construction*, and the concert was a success.

}

It was easier to avoid thinking about Richard during the summer because I didn't have to see him. With no lessons to give, he had no reason to be at school. But the anxiety I had, the fear that he would end up shunning me, never really left. That summer, I began to develop an obsession with a girl whose situation resembled my own.

I had always worshipped the women in my midst whose determination and focus and control shamed me because they seemed to be working harder than I was — the ballerinas of the New York City Ballet. Anyone living on the Upper West Side saw them, women thinner than a Saturday *New York Times* in August, women who, while walking north, had feet pointing nearly east and west. They waited in line at the Chemical Bank, picked out salads at the Korean market, walked to and from the New York State Theater where they worked, hair caught in high ponytails swinging from side to side.

If they had taken the time to study Juilliard musicians, I imagine they would have seen us the way we saw our "regular" college peers — kids who watched TV and wasted time. They came to Juilliard to teach at the School of American Ballet, and every time I passed one in the hall I would get a queasy feeling, a reminder that I could always work harder. I knew it was the time limit on their sculpted bodies that made succeeding early more urgent for them than for us. I didn't care. I wanted to be as focused as they were. I knew what it took for them to get there — the sweating, starving, barfing, bloody toes, and self-doubt — but I only saw the beauty of what they'd achieved.

One of these dancers was Suzanne Farrell. Now nearing the end of her career with the New York City Ballet, Farrell was one of the great American ballerinas. She was the muse of choreographer George Balanchine, who had founded the NYCB and led it until his death in 1983. And though he was 41 years her senior and married, he'd fallen in love with her.

I liked to picture her in the studio. I imagined her in a leotard and leg warmers, at first trying to fit in, later trying to stand out. She joined the company at 16 and by the late 1960s was Balanchine's all-consuming inspiration. She left the company for five years, dancing in Europe and then returning to the NYCB. But it was the time before the break, the years when she was the focus of his attention, that's what I wanted to know about. I thought about her dancing alone in the studio, dealing with the burden and the thrill of being adored, and dreading what would happen if she crossed him.

What unnerved me as I read about her was that she seemed to have loved him, too. Maybe she didn't love him the way he wanted, not enough to marry him, not even after he'd divorced his fourth wife to be with her, but it did seem she loved him. I looked at Richard and saw someone my grandfather's age. She looked at Balanchine and thought maybe there was romance. That's what made me anxious; I had to confront the possibility that someone my age could be attracted to someone 40 years older. I thought it was absurd, but there was a reason Richard didn't. Sometimes it happened.

That summer, I got involved with Ethan. I was available, he was free, and we were spending time together for the MOMA concert. I was attracted to him because he was smart and because he was attracted to me. In my head, this was a logical equation that made me feel like *I* was smart. He was also twice my age and a teacher at school. The difference between my relationship with him and the one with Richard was obvious to me — Ethan was not *my* teacher. He didn't have power over me. He couldn't make a call and get me an invitation directly to a semifinal round of an audition, couldn't suggest I get hired as an extra for an orchestra, and wouldn't be writing me any letters of recommendation. The question I never asked myself — was the only real difference that I welcomed a relationship with Ethan but not one with Richard? What if, like Suzanne Farrell with Balanchine, I'd been in love with Richard? Would Richard still be wrong for telling me he loved me?

I also never questioned why I kept my relationship with Ethan a secret. If it was conventional, why did he make it clear that no one at school should know? We had a beer at a back table at the Mayflower Hotel; we ate at restaurants way down in the Village or over on the East Side; when I spent the night, I walked to his apartment along Central Park West instead of taking the more direct path that crossed in front of Juilliard. I told no one.

Meanwhile, I read everything I could about Suzanne Farrell and George Balanchine. He'd been dead for three years by this point, but she was still in New York, dancing less frequently but still in the company. I was aware there were differences: she was a star and she had feelings for Balanchine that I would never have for Richard. Still, I wanted guidance. I was desperately anxious and wanted to know that my situation would not end badly.

There was no comfort to be found in her story. The reason Suzanne Farrell had left the company was because she crossed Balanchine — she married a young dancer within the company. She still danced important roles, but Balanchine took out his fury on her new husband. In a company that was very much a dictatorship, Farrell's husband found himself at the mercy of her jealous former love. He was not cast in roles he felt he should've been; Balanchine even requested he not come to work. Eventually, Suzanne and her husband brought the situation to a head, demanding he dance a particular role, and that was the end. They left. They spent five years with another company in Europe before she and Balanchine reconciled and she began dancing with him again. Her husband did not return to New York City Ballet.

⁊

Outside, it was the beginning of the end of summer. Inside Juilliard it was hard to say, the air could have been June's or July's. It had blown in off the Hudson, mixed with dirt and exhaust, and slowly worked its way into circulation in the school's halls. I was no longer alone all day — old students were returning and some new students were appearing, ones I didn't want to bother getting to know. I was practicing xylophone in the hall one day when the timpani teacher, Donald, came by. He disappeared into his studio. A few minutes later I heard his door open and he stood next to me at the xylophone, asking if I'd seen Sebastian. He wanted to set up lesson times with him.

Donald was going to be Sebastian's new teacher. Without telling him, Richard had dropped Sebastian as a student. Richard had arranged with Donald to have him take over as Sebastian's teacher and gave him the responsibility of telling Sebastian.

16
Quitting

Richard had broken up with Sebastian. I assumed it was because of me and I assumed that's what Sebastian thought, too. I never asked Richard and I never talked to Sebastian about it. It was one more thing to not discuss. When Richard came to school to teach now, he would pass Sebastian as if he didn't exist. I witnessed it a few painful times: a group of students standing in our narrow hallway, and along came Richard wearing his overcoat and news-boy cap, carrying his two-handled bag. Everyone would say hi, including Sebastian, but Richard's demeanor was a qualified cheerful; he smiled only in the direction of those who were not near Sebastian, pointedly refusing to show a real grin anywhere that it might fall on Sebastian. He did his peculiar sideways shuffle, not letting any part of himself get too close to Sebastian's orbit.

A few days into my fifth year, I knew that returning had been a mistake. Sebastian and I had broken up; Richard had dumped Sebastian. I had a relationship with Ethan but no one knew about it. And Caroline was gone.

She was still in New York and had very quickly become one of the freelancers who was doing the best work. But now when I showed up at eight in the morning and sat on the bench, I was alone. I didn't have any desire to get to know the new students, most of whom were still marveling at their fat acceptance letters and basking in the glow of the gold lettering on the side of the building that spelled out The Juilliard School.

Juilliard itself was also changing. Our new president was making ominous statements, talking about building a dorm (which sounded to me like coddling) and about the need for students to be able to talk intelligently about music. That would be fine if my goal was to dabble in percussion and then become the president of a music school, but it would do nothing for me at an audition. Somehow I'd also missed the fact that these new requirements would keep all master's students at school for two years, even those of us who were Juilliard bachelors.

Two more years. I couldn't do it.

I didn't tell Richard I was going to leave. I was afraid. Every week we still had our lesson, every week we went to dinner, but now he was quieter. I chattered furiously throughout the meal, trying to leave no room for us to talk about anything but music. I would wait out the semester, find a new place to practice, and then I would leave. Caroline had a practice studio down on Eighth Avenue, near the Port Authority bus terminal. That was the only place in Manhattan where you could actually make noise. I would ask her if she knew of an empty studio in the building.

Having made the decision to leave, I dropped any pretense of going to class and concentrated only on what mattered. I'd started studying full-time with Donald as well as Richard because I needed to confront my timpani playing. If playing a triangle part in orchestra caused me extreme anxiety, being assigned a timpani part made me wish I were dead. I would see the assignments on the bulletin board, my name spelled out in Moretti's block writing under "Timpani," and I would get anxious just looking at it. I tried all the usual tricks for working out the fear — get the part from the library, make my own copy of it, go to the library and write in cues, practice the part with the recording. The problem was, none of those things were the problem.

The problem was pitch. All the way back to fourth grade, back to my one percent on the "melody" section of the music test, understanding the intricacies of pitch had been a problem for me and hadn't gotten any better. Back then I wasn't even self-conscious about it. Pitch was such a mystery I didn't know how far out of tune I was. In my collection of albums I still had one from seventh-grade All-State Band on which I'd played timpani on Tchaikovsky's *March Slave*. There's a solo in the middle of the piece, just two notes back and forth for two measures. The interval between those two pitches was supposed to be a perfect fourth — it should have sounded like the first two notes in "Here Comes the Bride." Instead, I banged out the interval you hear when an ambulance goes by. I had no idea it was wrong.

There were many pitched instruments in the percussion family — xylophone, bells, vibraphone, marimba, chimes — but those pitches were already there and the challenge lay in hitting the right ones. Timpani was different: a big head of calf skin or plastic stretched across the top of what looked like a giant copper soup bowl, connected by rods to a foot pedal. Push the pedal forward, the head got tighter and the pitch higher. Release it backwards and it got looser and lower. Some pieces called for dozens of changes on each drum. If I plunked a set of timpani down in the middle of a vast cornfield where not a single pitched sound could distract me, I might come close to being able to tune. If I tried to change pitches while playing in a concert, surrounded by the cacophony of a symphony orchestra, the result was sometimes frightful.

Before the summer, Richard and I talked about the problem. Again, he compared me to Caroline. "I know she doesn't want to become a timpanist," he said, "and she certainly doesn't have to. But I say that knowing how she plays timpani." I had to be a decent timpani player before I could dismiss it.

{

My equivalent of an education seminar that semester was going to be playing at the Met. *The* Metropolitan Opera. They needed 12 extra percussionists for Wagner's *Das Rheingold*, and Caroline and I had been hired. Technically, we weren't playing with the orchestra. There were two sections in the opera where 12 of us would provide the sounds of metal forging — playing a rhythm on anvils that were set up at four stations hidden backstage. We would follow the conductor on TV monitors.

Opera was its own world within classical music. We didn't study it much at school — we were focused on symphonic repertoire and playing onstage. Our first entrance in *Rheingold* was an hour into the opera, and afterward, during the 20 minutes before the second entrance, I could stay backstage and watch. From this spot I was closer to the singers than the patrons in the front row. The voices I was hearing from ten feet away were trained to carry out to more than 3,000 members of the audience. They were *deafening*. They were like sound weapons. Sometimes they would soar over the sound of the orchestra, sometimes they would just bury them. A good tenor could flatten the whole orchestra with one held note. Along with the notes came great sheets of spit, backlit by the footlights.

The potential for disaster was enormous; it shamed the mere percussion ensemble concert. The singers lugged their considerable weight around on top of castles and ladders and boats. They disappeared through trapdoors. The traditional opera themes — lying, cheating, stealing, patricide, fratricide, suicide — all were occasions for singers to arm themselves with swords, guns, and knives. This kind of drama was a great distraction from school. I had the thrill of walking across 65th Street and heading down the ramp into the underground parking garage to the stage door. I hadn't won the audition and it wasn't my orchestra, but for six amazing performances that October I got to pretend.

≀

At the end of the summer I'd made a tape for the Columbus Symphony. Orchestras were getting so many résumés now that many began to require a tape as a preliminary audition. They would gather a committee together and have them listen to the tapes blindly — no one on the committee would know which tape belonged to which musician. If they thought your tape was good enough, they would invite you to the live preliminary round. It was a prelim to the prelim. Some people didn't have to make tapes, though. If your résumé was good enough, they might just invite you. Here was the problem: the only thing that really stood out on a résumé was orchestral experience, and to get orchestral experience you had to be playing in an orchestra. To get a job you had to have a job. So the orchestra musicians who wanted to audition for a better orchestra got invited. The rest of us had to make tapes.

My perfectionistic, controlling little heart was extremely excited. With a tape I could try, fall short, self-flagellate, try again. "Try again" was the problem. Unlike getting a 1600 on the SATs, perfection was not something you could really achieve by taping excerpts. It ended up being a question of time: how many takes of a long list of excerpts could you get down on tape?

I rented a pair of expensive microphones to use with my Walkman. I waited until the evening, put signs on the doors of 309 that said, *Recording — Do Not Knock*, and locked myself in the room. For three nights in a row, I taped. It was like being in a tomb. I set up the xylophone, warmed up, played through the excerpts slowly. I set up the metronome in my back pocket and ran the wire up to my ear, then walked over to the tape player and turned it on. I was shy when I called out, "Take one" or "Take 31." I would have to listen to my own voice when I played the tape back and it would sound strange. I played the excerpts over and over and over. After switching to the next instrument, I had to take some time to get the levels right. Play some loud and soft snare drum, then listen with headphones to make sure the soft wasn't covered with tape hiss and the loud wasn't distorted. Be sure the sound of the metronome running through my earpiece didn't come through on the tape. Rationalize, again, that using a metronome wasn't cheating. The Columbus Symphony wasn't going to know if I could keep steady time on my own. I didn't care. If another drummer told me he hadn't used a metronome for making a tape, I would think he was a liar or stupid.

I spent three days recording, then returned the microphones. Given that I was not naturally gifted in things electronic, a cautious me would have held on to the mikes until the final tape was in the mail. But I had always felt that the faster I moved, the more I would get done. Back in my room, listening to all the takes, I picked the best example of each excerpt. "Best" was the cleanest one with no obvious mistakes, certainly no wrong notes, the softest, or the loudest, or the one with the greatest range from soft to loud, and one that was stylistically appropriate, with beautiful phrasing. When I had made all the choices, I recorded them in order, going from one Walkman to another and adding a second generation of tape hiss in the process. While transferring the excerpts to the final tape, I erased three of them.

I had no time to chastise myself for my idiocy because the deadline was getting close. My "second-best" takes were not good enough, I decided, so I went back to rent the mikes again (the clerk pitied me my stupidity and didn't charge me), sealed myself in room 309 for a fourth evening, rerecorded the three excerpts, then carefully transferred the best takes to the master.

The Columbus Symphony thought it was good enough.

≀

In October, it was time to go. Columbus would be my second audition, but the first for which I had to travel.

For the Met audition, I hadn't given much thought to the art of packing; I knew if I forgot something I would only have to run back across the street. Now I planned out my plane trip with military precision. I would be flying with my snare drum packed inside a hard-shell case surrounded by wadded underwear and socks then checked underneath the plane, two pairs of cymbals with my dress pants and shirt layered between them and stored in the overhead bin, and a soft bag that didn't fit under the seat in front of me and had to be covered with a blanket when the stewardess went by. It contained two tambourines, a triangle and triangle beaters, marimba mallets, bell mallets, vibraphone mallets, xylophone mallets, snare-drum sticks and bass-drum beaters, a disassembled snare-drum stand, music, a practice pad, castanets, and my Walkman. In my jacket pocket was my prescription bottle of Inderal.

It was ten p.m. when the plane arrived in Columbus; the terminal was nearly empty. The New Yorkers disembarking ran toward "Ground Transportation," unable to stop competing for resources even in the midwest, where cabs were plentiful. I would have joined them out of habit but I was busy discovering that there were no porters around and I was going to have to carry all my instruments myself. Later, in my hotel room, I sat on the bed curling and uncurling my fingers, hoping they wouldn't still feel like claws the next day.

In the morning, I took a cab to the school, where we were told to meet. I passed several drummers walking from the hotel, pulling luggage carts with instruments secured with bungee cords.

Oh.

There were only going to be 41 of us, a small number for an open audition, and we'd all been told to arrive at nine a.m. Columbus was one of the smaller full-time orchestras. That still meant there would be 40 losers, and only if the audition went well. Sometimes, for whatever reason, a committee didn't do a good job of narrowing down the field throughout the prelims and semis. Then at the finals they couldn't agree on whom to hire. They could decide to choose no one, and no matter how much we complained about it (the orchestra was messed up; they had great players to choose from; how could they possibly have found no one good enough?) all of us would show up again a few months or a year later, when they held the audition a second time.

There was a monitor at the door, checking us in, casually drinking her coffee. If I had added caffeine to my system at that moment, it would have killed me. She gave me a number and returned my tape. I would be given an individual warm-up room 15 minutes before I played — until then I would be waiting in the group warm-up room.

Forty drummers in a room with curtains and carpeting would've been loud enough. What I walked into instead was the school's gym. There was a raised stage at one end and basketball-court lines on the floor. Most of us knew that protocol meant playing on a pad or at least softly on snare drum or tambourine. But in a room the size of a barn, with high ceilings and wood floors, the few who didn't know or didn't care, or who considered it a tactic to pummel the rest of us, filled the room with noise. It was deafening.

Even with all of us crowded into one room, I could see there were fewer drummers at this audition than at most. Maybe the tapes had discouraged some. Trying to make a tape while at a summer festival would not have been easy.

I unpacked, starting with my Walkman and headphones, and looked around for faces I recognized. I saw students I knew from the Cleveland Institute, Curtis Institute, Eastman. I saw a Temple student I knew from Interlochen. He'd been in the university division while I was still in the high school division and had beaten me in the camp's concerto competition.

With so much equipment, even the short trip from the gym to the warm-up room to the stage had to be thought out. I had to be able to carry everything myself: cymbals and one tambourine would go in a bag over one shoulder, a stick bag over the other, my snare drum on its stand with the other tambourine inverted on top, holding castanets and triangle. I sat against the wall, listening to ragtime music on my Walkman, and did some calculations.

The auditions started at ten and were scheduled for six an hour: eight minutes of playing with two minutes for getting in and out of the room. I was number seven. That meant taking one pill now, another 20 milligrams at nine forty-five, and another at about ten. Sixty milligrams would be enough to keep my hands steady, keep my heart from erupting through my chest wall. This wasn't counting the 20 milligrams I took the moment I woke up; I didn't want my pulse ever to get up to the level it had before the Met audition.

It was a strange formula I had. The stakes at an audition were so high, one of only a few chances a year to get a job, but I felt more threatened playing in front of an audience. In a concert, I risked humiliating myself in front of actual people. They would crane their necks to see the spectacle if I vomited onstage due to fright. If I fell apart today, behind the screen, the committee would only know that "number seven" had choked. I went to the bathroom to count out the pills, leaning my head under the faucet to swallow one. Two more went in my pocket.

When the monitor came to take me to a warm-up room, I was calm and prepared. Not just for an audition. I'd so overridden my natural response to fear, I could have opened a closet door in a dark room while scary music played in the background, all without my pulse breaking 60.

In the warm-up room I was handed a list of the excerpts that would be required in this preliminary round. They'd narrowed the list from two pages of possible excerpts to just eight short passages. It streamlined the process — we could take just the mallets and instruments we needed for those eight excerpts and leave the rest in the warm-up room. Two guys I didn't know lurked in the hall, trying to listen to what I was practicing so they could get a head start.

At 11:05 I was delivered to the personnel manager. He led me onstage and introduced me as candidate number seven. This time I was facing a sight I'd seen before: the screen separating me from the committee, the instruments in one straight line. This time I was prepared for that great gaping silence that opened up after I'd set the tips of my sticks down on the snare-drum head and before I'd played the first soft notes of the audition.

Nine of the 41 of us made the cut. Hearing my name called as part of that group was my reason for living. If it hadn't been medically suppressed, my heart would've pounded out of my chest.

There was a long wait before the semis began. The committee needed time to eat. I left my instruments at the hall and walked around downtown Columbus, eating and trying to work off the first dose of Inderal before I had to start the second.

On a xylophone excerpt in this round, I stumbled and missed a few notes in a row. Instead of dwelling on it and letting it affect the rest of the audition, though, I managed to put it aside and concentrate on the next excerpt.

When they announced the four who made the finals, I wasn't one of them. I was out of the running.

Still, it was progress. When I got back to school and was asked about the audition, I could say I'd made the semis. Columbus was my second audition and first minor success, and for the guy from Temple who'd beaten me in the concerto competition five years earlier, it was a job.

17
Deliverance

It was about this time that I began to think I might be losing it. Not stand-in-a-corner-and-crash-two-pieces-of-metal-together crazy but Bellevue crazy. I was anxious all the time. There was so much that I was not thinking about that, in fact, I spent a lot of energy not thinking. I needed all the space in my head to be occupied with learning and practicing, and instead it was filled with worry.

There are many reasons why musicians eventually give up. There are rare instances in which a musician wins the first audition he takes, but for most of us taking auditions was a process. There would be many, many times we didn't win before we got lucky. I'd heard about a flute player who took 21 auditions before she won one. Through 20 losses she kept believing, kept practicing, kept playing the solo in Ravel's *Daphnis et Chloé*, over and over, trying to make it perfect yet keep it sounding fresh. It was hard work, but the work was not the hard part. If I knew for sure I would win the 50th audition I took, it would only be a matter of surviving the process.

But it's the uncertainty — the not knowing when, or if, it'll ever happen — that is hardest to accept. How do you plan a life when you have one big unanswered question?

It was easy to continue believing in ourselves through school. Four years, even the five or six it took to get a bachelor's and master's, felt reasonable — most of our friends from high school were in college, too. Almost all of us had parents paying the bills for those years. We might've been living in crappy dumps, but we didn't trouble ourselves with how to pay the rent on them.

After school was when it got hard. I thought about the drummers who'd been with me at school and graduated before me. Two were playing in the Honolulu Symphony, which at the time was a good entry-level orchestra. Two, including Caroline, were doing the kind of freelancing that meant satisfying playing and good pay. There were others who were doing another kind of freelancing: essentially treading water, cobbling together teaching and playing crappy gigs, some living like paupers. I knew another two who'd already quit music. I imagined that some who were currently hanging on would eventually join them.

I tried not to think about my own limit. I could not imagine that I would never get an orchestra job. I figured that if I kept improving — making semis or the finals at auditions — I would have the momentum I needed to go on. I had only vague thoughts of how I would be supporting myself, something my parents would expect once I left school in six weeks. I was going to have to work at some kind of retail job and take any gigs I could to support my practice habit. I was so desperate to leave school, I was willing to become just one more unemployed musician.

Something like salvation came along just then. A bassoonist at school had told me about an orchestra being formed in Miami called the New World Symphony. A full orchestra's worth of musicians, ages 21 to 30, would live together in a hotel on the beach, get free rent and $300 a week, play concerts, and practice. It sounded like a year-round Colorado Phil. Every few years a conductor would get it in his head to try to create a training orchestra like this, a place for some of the many jobless conservatory graduates to get experience while they took auditions. It had never worked. There had been one in New York — the National Orchestral Association — but the pay was so bad that the musicians needed other work as well and couldn't concentrate on playing. Free rent and $300 a week sounded good — enough to live on but not too much. We would have neither the distraction of needing to earn money to eat nor the distraction of earning so much we could shop and have hobbies. Living next door to other musicians meant being able to fall out of bed in the morning and practice where you stood. No one could complain since they were about to do the same thing. I wouldn't have to try to find practice space in New York. More importantly, I would have colleagues. That's what had worried me most about leaving school. We learned as much from each other as we did from our teachers. We competed, criticized, and goaded one another.

They were holding auditions for New World at Juilliard and most of the other big conservatories around the country. Four percussionists would be asked to join.

Having just gone through the Columbus audition, I was relaxed for this one. Not Inderal-free, but relaxed. I set up in Donald's room and played through the list for two musicians, men who were going to be administrators in the new orchestra. That was it. They took notes and filed away my performance for comparison. Then I waited.

When the New World Symphony called and invited me to join, the relief I felt was greater than playing all the way through *Porgy* without hitting a wrong note. It was a farm team, a temporary job, but it was a job and it was progress. If the orchestra succeeded beyond the initial three months, each musician would be allowed to stay another three years. The rumor was that New World was going to be heavily supported by a shipping magnate. It seemed likely I could stay in the orchestra long enough to get a permanent job.

I told my parents and friends I would be going to Miami at the beginning of January. I hadn't told Richard because I was afraid to. I had never told him I was leaving school after the semester ended, and now I didn't tell him I was leaving for Miami. Of course, I was supposed to. Though it wasn't for a permanent job, I'd won a competitive audition. I would be paid money to play in an orchestra, and that was the point of taking lessons and practicing and everything I'd done at Juilliard for more than four years. I wanted to put on the glasses through which I could see my situation as it should be: Richard the teacher, proud that I had won; I the student, running to tell him the news before anyone else. Instead, I avoided telling him. A week passed, then another, and still I hadn't told him. Finally, he heard the news from someone else.

Sitting on the bench in the hall, waiting for my final lesson, I distracted myself by daydreaming about Miami. Sweat, palm trees, old people, the beach. Weekly paychecks in the incredible amount of $300. Famous conductors, daily rehearsals, concerts every week. A set of crutches leaned on the bench beside me: the week before, while walking in front of 67th Street Wines (a store inexplicably located on the corner of Columbus and 68th Street), I'd slipped on some ice and broken my leg. I was lucky — only arms, wrists, and hands mattered to me.

The student whose lesson preceded mine came out of Richard's room. I'd dreaded that sound even at Eastman precollege — the heavy door being pulled open that meant it was my turn to step up and prove myself. I tucked my crutches under my arms and gimped toward the studio.

Inside, Richard was slumped on his stool. His head was bowed, and when I came in he turned it sideways to look at me. Instead of sitting in his usual spot near the speaker, his stool faced the couch. I took my time limping across the room. There was a throw pillow on the couch and I propped my cast on it.

I knew we would only be talking, yet I'd still brought my sticks and pad, music and a metronome. I needed my props. They sat on the floor by my good foot, the only place I could reach to put them.

I was too anxious to wait for Richard to start. "I'm sorry," I said. I began to justify not telling him right away. I was trying to explain that I'd been struggling with the decision — whether or not to go to Miami. We both knew I would not have passed up the opportunity. Play in a nearly professional orchestra or sit on my futon and wait for the Westchester Symphony to call? Did I think raising the pitch of my voice made me sound more sincere? By the end of my speech, I was nearly squealing.

"I heard you were going to leave anyway," Richard said.

"Yes. I really couldn't take my parents' money anymore." This was another excuse I'd invented to justify why I'd been ready to leave school even before New World had come along.

"You *chose* not to."

"No, I really could not take it anymore."

"You *chose* not to."

Why did it matter? I was going to Miami. "I chose not to," I said. "I chose not to take it anymore."

"Are you leaving because of someone at school?"

He meant Sebastian.

"No."

Richard looked at his hands. They rested on his thighs, fleshy palms up. I looked at the bald dome of his ducked head. There was nothing else to say.

⁊

We tended not to talk, at Juilliard, about how music made us "feel," about how it could thrill us or make us cry. But Donald talked about it. One of the reasons he was a great musician was that he felt so much so deeply.

When I was learning Schumann's Second Symphony with him, he stood across the drums from me while we discussed some of the technical aspects of playing the piece. As the Cleveland Orchestra came through the speakers behind us, he also wanted to share his feelings with me. He wanted to tell me how much he loved this music.

"These Schumann symphonies are like four gems," he said that day. Then, leaning across the timpani and drawing me in, as if what he was about to say was a secret, he whispered, "But this one shines a little brighter."

I had a final lesson with him on the same day as my final lesson with Richard. Somehow he knew that the sadness and exhaustion I was carrying had nothing to do with my broken leg. I sat on a stool and started to cry. "It's normal to tell your teacher that you've won a job," he said. "But I think he's just sad that you're leaving." He leaned across the drums toward me. "You know," he said, lifting his elbows and cupping his hands toward his face, another of his gestures that defined him for us, "when you break a bone and it heals, it's stronger than it was before."

꒳

Because I was due to get my cast off two days before the orchestra started rehearsing, the last New World musician to arrive in Miami was going to be me. The day before I left, a doctor removed my cast, and when the first members of the orchestra were just starting to show up in Miami and fight for the best rooms, I took a walk across the park. My newly liberated leg was a wasted little stick, hardly bigger than my shinbone itself, and quite hairy. I put on my duck boots, the first time I'd worn two shoes in six weeks, and set off for the West Side.

About a foot of snow had fallen the night before, and by the time I entered the park on 67th Street, the bottoms of my pants were soaked. I limped along the sidewalk, passing the statue of Balto, the sled dog whose ears had been rubbed gold from little kids' hands. There were no markers in the park, but I always thought of certain parts of it as belonging to one side or the other. Balto, the Carousel, the Boathouse, the sad zoo — to me they all belonged to the East Side, just as surely as Fifth Avenue did. The Sheep Meadow, the baseball diamonds — they were ours, the West Side's, not just in proximity but in attitude. Tavern on the Green belonged to the tourists. A few weeks before, I had suggested to Ethan we go there. He was appalled that I didn't know it wasn't a restaurant for New Yorkers.

I had just said good-bye to Ethan that morning before my appointment. I would've been sad about having another breakup but like everything else that wasn't convenient to think about, I was in denial. I could pretend we might be a couple in the future just to avoid thinking about it now and admitting to myself that it was over.

I walked on the side of the looping road that ran through the park. The snow had been cleared more recently there than on the pathways, and it was easier to drag my bad leg than lift it up and out of the snow with each step. Cars sped past, mostly cabs, heading downtown. On Saturdays and Sundays the drive was closed to traffic. In the summer, bikers, skaters, and joggers took over.

Nobody was lingering on the road right now. Everyone who passed me on foot seemed in a hurry, just using the park to cut from one part of town to the other. I passed the Sheep Meadow, where Caroline and I had sunbathed, where Sebastian and I had played Frisbee. I was leaving both of them behind. Caroline was staying in New York, a working professional musician. Sebastian had another semester of school, then two more years if he stayed for a master's. I didn't know what he would do after that, but I assumed I would see him at auditions.

Just before leaving the park, I passed through Strawberry Fields, the area designed by Yoko Ono to honor her husband. It was just steps from where he'd lived and died. At the center of the field stood a stone inscribed with the word *Imagine*. I imagined John

Lennon wondering what he might have accomplished if some crazy asshole hadn't shot him. Two red roses lay on the stone.

I came out of the park at 72nd Street and headed downtown toward Juilliard. I had said good-bye to Richard weeks earlier, just before school let out for Christmas vacation. We had hugged. Still framing the conversation the way it ought it be instead of the way it was, I said I'd be sure to write and tell him about my new colleagues and about all that I was playing in the orchestra. There had been no resolution, but the relief I felt in leaving was tremendous.

Walking through the double glass doors to the school, I realized even this entrance wouldn't be here for much longer. The president in the perfect suit was changing the entrance of the school from 66th Street, in the shadow of the Chinese embassy, to the Grand Plaza overpass of Lincoln Center. Soon the dorm would rise between the school and the West Side Highway, and students would be moving in, fighting over the rooms with views of the Hudson.

Juilliard was becoming a different place. I'd added my exhalations to the corners and now it was time to go.

18
Brave New World

If Juilliard was a narrow, insular, incestuous group of "artists," practicing, competing, and performing in the same square block, it had nothing on the New World Symphony. Juilliard's ranks included dancers and actors, and musicians who hoped to become soloists or play chamber music. To funnel ourselves any more narrowly than Juilliard, we would have to take all the aspiring orchestral musicians and put ourselves on an island.

That is what New World did.

During the sweat and stink of a January weekend, 95 of us arrived at our new home. The Plymouth Hotel on Miami Beach was a grand art-deco structure with the emphasis on *was*; pink and baby blue, it was dying of neglect as surely as the older residents with whom we shared our space. Though the orchestra had bought the place for us, they hadn't gotten around to kicking out all the old people.

New World was an experiment. Conductor Michael Tilson Thomas had used his charisma and energy to create a symphony orchestra where none had existed. None of us — investors, administrators, musicians — knew if this would work. But for those of us who managed to get in, giving up our lives to go south was easy. There were so few options for conservatory graduates who wanted to get orchestra jobs that a thousand musicians had auditioned.

Right from the beginning, New World was a cozy cocoon for the larval musicians who were lucky enough to land there. Being the last musician to arrive at the Plymouth, I was given the room with the overwhelming stench of sewer gas brewing in my cauldron of a toilet. I could not have cared less. *I had my own toilet.* The fire-engine-red front door of my apartment led to a room with a kitchenette lining one wall. I had a Formica table, a vinyl chair, a dresser, and industrial carpeting; I had a bed infested with some kind of cooties that made me itch, I had three-inch-long roaches — palmetto bugs. And all this was free. The only work we had to do to earn our room and $300 a week was the one thing we wanted to do anyway — practice and play in the orchestra.

I had even secured a practice room. There was a recreation center nearby and the next day we would start having rehearsals there, preparing for our inaugural concert. I asked for a key, then filled a storage closet with instruments. Now I could roll out of my infested bed and walk the two blocks to my personal practice space, marveling along the way at the sun's reflection off my blindingly white legs.

There was one other advantage to being sequestered here, marooned with my fellow castaways: to be better than the competition, you had to know exactly how good that competition was. In New York I would've been surrounded by musicians, but not all of them would be auditioning for jobs. Taking auditions was the point where music and sporting events intersected. I could practice the bell part to *The Sorcerer's Apprentice* until I could play it accurately at a blazingly fast tempo. It would sound impressive only until candidate number 50 played right after me and played it faster. I couldn't have conjured a situation more perfect than New World for keeping the pressure up — we were going to perform together, practice together, even live together. Every day I would hear how the competition was doing.

{

The name New World suggested a pioneering adventure, and for all the conservatism involved in classical music, it did seem that we were breaking new ground. Gathered around me onstage at our first rehearsal were musicians from many of the top music schools. At 19 musicians, Juilliard had sent the largest contingent. I knew all three bassoon players — two had just been in school with me; the third, who I knew from my summer at Colorado Phil, was one of only a few married musicians at New World. Also from that summer in Evergreen was the viola player, Amy, and a violinist I'd sat behind for nine weeks and with whom I'd never exchanged a word. There was the trumpet player I knew from both Juilliard and Colorado who distinguished himself by playing great auditions and then falling apart in concerts. There was the cellist from California I'd met on the first day of Juilliard registration and hadn't talked to in the four-plus years since. Many of the low brass players had come from Indiana University — I'd never met anyone from that school. And in my own section, there were three other drummers.

Until now, I had somehow managed to avoid long-term exposure to drummers from other schools. It was at summer festivals where we cross-pollinated the most, but at both Waterloo and Colorado Phil, my sectionmates were all classmates. Of the three in this new section, I knew the most about Laura. She had gotten both her bachelor's and master's at Temple in Philadelphia — their students sometimes came up to Juilliard to audition for summer festivals. I'd seen her in the bathroom at school, warming up on a practice pad she'd balanced on the sink, and I met her, briefly, at the Columbus audition a few months before, when we had both made the semifinal round. Women drummers were still so outnumbered as to be memorable. She also stood out as a born-again. I'd met a few of those at Eastman — something about the pressures of conservatory life combined with the soul-sucking winters in Rochester made several students turn to Jesus. I took them less seriously as competitors because of their divided loyalties.

At 21, Doug was the youngest of my new colleagues. In this business, age was a subtle source of either tension or pride. Doug could not only claim to have gotten exactly where we had but more quickly (with the implicit understanding that by the time he was our age he would be further along than we were), but he also had left the Cleveland Institute a semester before getting his bachelor's. He was friendly and unguarded and blond and blue-eyed and — I would soon learn — very talented.

Then there was James. I'd met him for the first time the day before, out in front of the rec center, and if I'd been a dog I would have raised my hackles and peed on his car. He shook my hand and said it was nice to meet me, all the while staring at the ground. I looked at James and saw myself — wary, mistrustful, insecure, deeply competitive — packaged as a 26-year-old man. He'd also come from Cleveland, having just finished his master's. We were instantly, *thrillingly*, enemies.

New World had hired a personnel manager and a librarian, but no stage crew, so we drummers agreed to be our own crew for an extra $50 a week. With no training or muscles or special licenses, we started driving the 24-foot trucks to and from downtown Miami, loading and unloading our instruments. We had instruments — sent to us by our Yamaha sponsors — but no cases for them. Nor did we have dollies. We picked up timpani weighing hundreds of pounds each, and two of us together would waddle down the rec-center stairs with a drum between us. We'd balance the drum on the truck's lift and try to get it to the truck bed without chopping off any fingers.

We were disastrously bad at the job. During our first three months in Miami, we racked up an impressive number of incidents: forgot to padlock the roll-down door of the truck and had the contrabassoon stolen; after it was recovered from a local pawnshop, forgot to lock the side door of the truck's cargo area and had it stolen *again*; forgot that a truck is tall as well as wide and cleanly picked off the decorative light fixture hanging from a lamppost; backed up into and mowed over a different lamppost moored in concrete, remaining unaware until the post was bent nearly in half; and finally, James, driving on his own, had made a tight right turn and sent an unsuspecting car sideways up a nine-inch curb. Despite the insurance claims, we were still such an economical choice that we were allowed to keep our jobs. The four of us got to rehearsals early to set up, stayed late to break down, then loaded ourselves four across in the truck's cab to drive between venues.

ʆ

On the podium was Michael Tilson Thomas. Here was our new boss looking very much like one of his charges: not a streak of gray in his hair, not an ounce of fat on his body. He wasn't one of us. Staggeringly talented, he'd just been appointed music director of the London Symphony Orchestra. He was 43 but had been conducting professionally since he'd stepped into the spotlight at 25. Behind him, in the audience, were members of the board and many of the patrons who'd brought us here, those who shared Michael's vision.

Why were we so thrilled to be here? We'd eagerly picked up our whole lives — quit school, gave up apartments, left relationships and steady day jobs — to move to a Miami that had declined into ruin. There would be an "after" — within about two years, the area would start becoming South Beach — but we were living in the "before." Most of us had grown up and attended schools in places where January was January and Florida was for vacations. Now we lived among prostitutes, drug dealers, and old Jewish couples on fixed incomes. I spent some late nights on the back patio of the Plymouth with the two Johns and Amy, the four of us drinking beer, a stereo speaker pointed out of John's bottom-floor window so we could hear "real" (not classical) music, wearing tank tops and shorts, and then, one night, stripping them off to go swimming in a pool filled with cloudy green water so dirty it made our eyes red.

Many of the nearby hotels were abandoned, including the one that backed up to the Plymouth. We made a drunken game of taking the corncobs from an earlier barbecue and throwing them through the broken windows of that hotel. We were surrounded by palmetto bugs; by a woman (formerly a man) named Jackie, who fed the hundreds of stray cats that lived in our neighborhood; by some homeless people, one of whom surprised a bass player named Brandon one night by trying to climb through the window of his first-floor room until Brandon pushed him back out; by the desk workers — José, who bobbed his head constantly; Mitch, whom we called "Lumpy" on account of the golf-ball-sized tumors underneath the skin of his forearms; and Sonja, whose face registered the toll of sun and cigarettes and who sounded like she was saying "sensimilla" when she was saying "Thanks a million."

All this for $300 a week and no guarantee that it would last beyond three months. Yet we had come because it was the best option we had. If I had stayed in New York, I would've quit school and then, untethered, I would be practicing aimlessly in the studio down by Port Authority. All my instruments would be crammed into a room that I would share with two or three or four others, the lot of us making up schedules so we all got enough time. Then I would have set about earning a living in some way that wouldn't depress me so much I'd want to quit music. If I was lucky and worked hard, I might get some freelancing; in the meantime, I'd double my hours selling kids' clothes.

Just like the ex-Juilliard horn player I'd come across my first week in New York, I'd make a routine for myself as a distraction from my depressing circumstances; wake up in my fake apartment, shower in my shared bathroom, skip breakfast to save money, walk the 40 blocks to my studio to save more money, practice for four hours until the rock-and-roll drummer stumbled in for his session, work for four hours at the kids' clothing store, contemplate throughout the dreary afternoon how different it felt to work in retail when you're relying on it for a living wage, eat grapes for dinner, hole up in my "apartment" and listen to music, try to practice anything soft enough to get away with: practice pad, soft snare-drum rolls, soft tambourine thumb rolls, until my neighbor knocked politely on the wall; and finally, before going to sleep, place a call to my parents asking for the $310 to cover my rent for that month.

In Miami, we were surrounded by circumstances we never would have imagined in our wildest upper-middle-class dreams (culminating a few years hence, when a pair of legs connected only to a torso was discovered in a dumpster next to the Plymouth). But we knew we were lucky to be here. We played music, we practiced, and we got paid. Until — *unless* — I could win an audition, this was the best place I could be.

≀

With pomp, circumstance, and fanfare, the New World Symphony gave its inaugural concert on February 4, 1988, at the Gusman Center. It was theater and rightfully so. For a city that, until that moment, had not supported a symphony orchestra, it was an incredible accomplishment. Instead of sitting onstage, waiting for the concertmaster to come out and tune, the whole orchestra walked out to a standing ovation. Then Michael came out and we played Brahms's *Academic Festival Overture*, a nod to the group's mission. We played a premiere written by Charles Wuorinen for the occasion entitled *Bamboula Beach* and finished the concert with Beethoven's Symphony No. 5.

If the expense and lavishness of the post-performance party was any indication, the concert was a success. From the Gusman Center, we went to the CenTrust building, the iconic I. M. Pei structure, and on the 11th-floor skydeck ate and drank like the college kids we had recently been.

The next day, the newspapers in Miami and Fort Lauderdale rendered their verdicts. "The New World Symphony made an impressive debut Thursday evening at Miami's Gusman Cultural Center," the *Sun-Sentinel* said, "living up to much of the ballyhoo surrounding its inauguration." The *Herald* said we were "in full spit and polish" and that "this orchestra is on its way up, with a leader of rare imagination and ability." Later in the *Sun-Sentinel* article, the critic pulled out his thesaurus and wrote, "It sounded Thursday as an ensemble should . . . confident, dynamic, cohesive, disciplined, fully attentive to musical and technical details." He added, "Of course, cockiness is a trademark of young orchestras, and the New World Symphony gives every indication of being one of the cockiest."

}

Cocky was becoming a problem for me.

James and I were not the only two in the section who didn't understand each other. Laura was religious, I was a heathen; Doug was friendly, I'd just left New York. Most of all, however, they had not spent the last four and a half years in the confines of Juilliard. When surrounded by like-minded bullheads at Juilliard, I not only didn't stand out, I was the weakest member. Caroline and Sebastian had been utterly fearless. In Miami, I found that I had become the new Caroline and Sebastian.

If my first job had been in a regular orchestra and not a training group, there would've been an established order and my job would be to conform to the customs of that orchestra in order to get tenure. At New World, we had no tradition. For instance, no one was in charge of assigning parts. At school, we'd had an associate dean; in a regular orchestra, there would be a principal who would get paid extra to assign the parts. Before our first rehearsal here in Miami, we'd gotten together with the aim of dividing parts. I think the intention of the other three was for us to divide the parts fairly, each of us speaking up in turn about the parts we most wanted to play. Another way: the biggest bully (me) could just tell the others what she wanted to play, forcing their stunned selves to either speak up and object, or agree and thus begin a long, slow, simmering boil.

Another problem was learning to play together. When we were toddlers, learning to "play together" meant sharing toys. Now, in the context of our new job, it meant learning to adjust. Tempos, dynamics, pitch — all were up for discussion. Since there was no established tradition, it fell to the conductor to try to guide us. It was a free-for-all.

There were as many opinions about *where* to play as there were players. If the lot of us had been playing with a giant metronome, the answer would be "whenever that big machine clicks." No room for interpretation. But if there is a guy on a podium waving a stick, and 90 or so musicians sitting at varying distances from him trying to interpret at what point along each of his movements to play, the answer varies. Consider just the downbeat, the conductor's motion that starts the piece. He's probably starting by holding the baton somewhere in the neighborhood of his shirt's third stud, about mid-chest level. Then he raises the baton, until it's about level with his mouth. During that upbeat, he and the orchestra breathe in. Then — chaos. All the way down, in the time it takes for his baton to travel from chin to belt line, musicians could play an entrance and fairly have said they played on the downbeat. But it didn't work that way. Majority ruled. If there was a nice resounding chord consisting of 90 percent of the orchestra playing at navel level, then a cymbal crash coming in at the top of the cummerbund would be "early." Wait until the appendectomy scar, and it would sound "late." Percussionists were prime targets for getting called out for being late, because we were at the back of the stage. Sound took just a little longer to reach the podium, long enough for the conductor to scream at us.

The New York orchestras had a reputation for playing on the early side of the beat. Left to their own devices, a group of musicians trained in New York would have finished a downbeat before the baton dropped past the conductor's collar. No discussion needed. This tradition may have come from the speed at which New Yorkers generally moved, which was fast, or it may have come from not wanting to appear to be afraid to be the first one in. My natural tendency was to play late, which is why I embraced this New York religion as only a convert can — I played early. It was drilled into me. I'd been yelled at countless times, by conductors in orchestra, by Caroline in percussion ensemble, to play more on top of the beat.

So even though there was great ambiguity involved, I never framed my comments as opinions. As the bullied becomes the bully, I sat in the audience when I wasn't playing and then rendered my verdict to the rest of my section: *You're behind.* I told them that constantly. It's what I thought and it was also completely irrelevant. If Michael wasn't telling them they were behind, then it wasn't a problem. It was also not my job.

The morning of March 4, we were rehearsing Shostakovich's Tenth Symphony for a concert that night. The snare-drum part, especially in the second movement, was an excerpt — it was one of the many pieces we might have to play for an audition. That made it prime material. Doug was playing it, and he had already shown that he was a great snare drummer. I was playing bass drum, not the hardest part, but it certainly would have been wise for me to pay attention to that part which, after all, was the only part I was responsible for. Instead, I decided I would pay more attention to Doug's part. This was an "open rehearsal" — we'd invited patrons to sit in the audience but we were supposed to just ignore them and have a regular rehearsal. That never happened. If there was an audience, we were performing. We could fairly say that "open rehearsals" were neither open nor rehearsals. So we were showing off to pay back this particular group of patrons and make them feel special and privileged, and as we were performing the second movement, the head on Doug's snare drum broke. These heads, whose surface we relentlessly beat, were made of cowhide. The extreme humidity in Miami, which none of us was yet used to, caused the skin to expand and contract. Occasionally, one of our pointy little drumsticks went tearing through the hide.

Doug was mad. Fortunately for him, it happened right at the end of the rehearsal, but he still had to worry about finding another head for the concert. He had to wet up the head, put it on, and make sure it was tuned and ready to be abused a few hours later. Even if I had framed my comments as an opinion, it would not have been the right time to speak up. But I had been assuming that their silence over the last two months of working together meant that my section — at least Doug and Laura — welcomed my comments.

I began by telling Doug that he sounded good, but I didn't even wait to let the compliment sound genuine before I plowed on. Then I started to tell him it would sound even better if he pushed the tempo ahead and drove the orchestra.

Doug cut in. He looked as frustrated as I'd seen him look in our two months together, which to a New Yorker looked only like he was impatiently hailing a cab. "Well," he said, "I'm playing it the way I want to." And he left it at that.

Later that afternoon, I was in my room listening to the Shostakovich on my Walkman. In a few hours, those of us who didn't have cars would pile into the junkers of the few who did for the ride downtown. There was a knock on my door. It was Doug. He came into my room, cringing as he passed the bathroom. (I'd long since gotten used to the sewer-gas smell, but it hit my visitors like a slap in the face.) In his hand was the split snare-drum head. He pulled out one of my vinyl chairs and sat at my table.

As he cleared his throat and prepared to speak, I knew from his calm and serious manner that he wanted to discuss the morning's rehearsal. I also knew that even though he was a year younger than me, he was many dog years my senior in maturity. My bluff had been called.

He started by talking about the rehearsal, about how I'd gone on with my opinions about his playing even as he was obviously worrying about a replacement head. He then broadened the scope to include the entire time we'd been a section, saying that my way of constantly telling the rest of the section how to play "didn't really work" for him. He was as kind and mature as a radio psychologist. I was mortified. I couldn't wait for him to leave so I could cry.

Self-reflection did not occupy a lot of my time at this stage — any time I spent analyzing myself was given over to self-criticism about my playing. That night, however, I did think that although I might have been behaving appropriately for Juilliard, I was no longer there. Just as I had been lucky my first real experience with nerves had happened during a rehearsal, I was lucky I'd been called on my behavior here at New World. If I'd been enough of an ass to take that attitude to my first job, I might have been fired for it.

≀

Our first season ended with a declaration of success. Two of the orchestra's administrators sat us down one night in the rec center and told us the orchestra would continue in Miami in the fall. They even had work during the summer for us; we would have a residency at UC Irvine and in Big Sky, Montana. But first we would be subject to an evaluation and asked to stay or leave.

This was a dream situation for an orchestra; for the musicians it was yet another source of sphincter-clenching anxiety. In professional orchestras, strong tenure rules made it nearly impossible to fire musicians. These rules protected a great player to whom a conductor had taken an irrational dislike. The rule was also good for a musician who didn't prepare, stopped practicing, or generally descended into instrumental decrepitude — it was just terrible for the rest of the orchestra.

New World wasn't going to have that problem. In the evaluations, about a third of the musicians were either asked to leave or were put on probation. In theory this version of probation was vague, but in practice the message was clear: *Play better — there are hundreds of musicians who want to take your place.*

All four of us drummers were invited to stay. I could actually support myself by playing music. Not well — my parents still paid my health insurance, I didn't own a car, or actually anything beside records and instruments — but I had safely landed in a temporary job. Now it was time to concentrate on getting out.

19
Waiting for Auditions

If anxiety had been visiting me for the past few years, it now decided to move in and become a permanent resident. It sat quietly in the corner while I practiced, and when I got up it chased me out of the room. It didn't stop biting at my heels until I started practicing again. While I slept, it chewed on my stomach lining.

By this time, I was obsessing full-time: *Get a job.* And this kind of focus was not irrational, it was hyperrational. Witness, for instance, Debi Thomas, whom I watched skate that winter in the Calgary Olympics. The press pointed out that she was *good* at a lot of things: good student, good future doctor, good skater. Not *great.* I wondered what would have happened if she had devoted herself only to skating. She might've ended up on a higher podium, crying tears of a different kind down onto Katarina Witt's head.

By the beginning of our second season, they had kicked the last of the old people out of the Plymouth. I had enough seniority to receive a new room on the first floor, facing the murky depths of the pool. I listened to a baby wail through the first night, crying terribly. Like a good New Yorker, I kept my head down and didn't investigate; had I done so, I would have found out sooner that the inconsolable baby was actually a cat looking for a mate.

Now that there were no non-musicians within hearing distance, we were free to use our small apartments as full-time practice rooms. I was going to know other instruments' excerpts as well as I knew my own. I lived next to a trumpet player and heard the solo from *Petrushka* in all its renditions: good, bad, mediocre, proud, pathetic, triumphant. He practiced the beginning of Mahler 5, the stately march that opens Mussorgsky's *Pictures at an Exhibition*, the piercing beginnings of Copland's *Fanfare for the Common Man*. Over and over and over. Above me was a flute player, and through the bathroom vent I heard the solos from *Daphnis et Chloé*, *Bolero*, *Afternoon of a Faun*. I learned all too well what was hard for them to do. My shoulders tightened when they made a mistake, I bristled when their time didn't correspond with my foot-tapping, and I winced when they sat on a note that was too high. This was total and painful immersion. I could only imagine what it was like for them to have to listen to *me*.

A full-time timpanist joined the orchestra. Gary had gone to Cleveland, but I knew him from Interlochen and from the one year he spent at Juilliard. Freed from having to worry about timpani, Laura, Doug, James, and I went back to playing only percussion.

That fall, an audition was announced for the Cleveland Orchestra. One of the top orchestras in the country, the symphony was a polished gem in a crappy town. The city was justifiably proud of this institution

— this was, after all, Cleveland, and other than being able to buy a house for the price of a Porsche 911, there were few selling points. Their orchestra had long been more exclusive than others with regard to their auditions. No mass cattle calls for them; they only invited a select group whom they felt could actually do the job well. Considering that the job was for percussion/assistant timpani, it made sense that my lack of timpani experience would exclude me from this group. Still, I confused action with progress and after I received a rejection letter I brazenly called the personnel manager and asked if he would reconsider letting me audition. He bluntly told me I didn't have enough timpani experience. Cleveland had a style they wanted to perpetuate and tended to take their own students more seriously. Gary, James, and Doug were all invited. The three of them flew off to the audition and, as always, the results were broadcast through our inbred world long before they returned home. A Cleveland student, someone I hadn't heard of, got the job. James, Doug, and Gary had gotten nowhere, meaning they didn't get out of the prelims.

It would not be hard to describe the feelings I had when I heard that none of them had gotten the job, but it would be hard to admit those feelings. Quite uncharitable feelings, like a big breath of relief. Not so much for Gary, who was a timpanist, or James, who was leaning toward taking more timpani auditions, but for Doug. He had replaced Caroline and Sebastian as my daily competition. It wasn't that I was gleeful when my competitors didn't succeed, I was just momentarily slightly less terrified than if they had.

⁘

In October, we took a mini-tour of Florida. It was a great triumph for New World to be spreading the word of its success around the state. We were also pitted against the established orchestras in Florida. We played Mahler's Fifth Symphony in Tampa, home to the Florida Orchestra. The third movement of the Mahler was a showcase for the principal horn, which started and ended the movement, and had big, bold solos in between. The critic for the *St. Petersburg Times* wrote, "Can Santa send us the New World Symphony's horn section? The Florida Orchestra's section is mighty poor, and the New World's principal would sound great in any professional orchestra."

Putting a comment like that in print was the harshest possible job performance review I could imagine. I'd have lit the fire of my self-immolation with that paper if the criticism had been aimed at me. Back in Miami, we prepared some American music, rehearsing two of Charles Ives's symphonies, Bernstein's *Fancy Free* suite, and Steve Reich's *The Four Sections*, for which the composer himself came and coached us.

I was still taking Inderal — getting my prescription transferred to Miami Beach, I needed only to throw a drumstick in any direction to hit a pharmacy. My history with nerve problems had been so short — there was the very first inkling at my high school graduation recital, the fear leading up to the performance of "Frivolity," which unnerved me enough to talk to Richard about it, and my hand shaking while Caroline was watching me play triangle — just those three little cherry bombs and then the splitting of the atom during the Westchester rehearsal that caused me to turn to Inderal. Nothing in between that could be seen as an organic progression and let me understand where it would now go from here.

Throughout these months of perpetual sunshine, I began to get an idea of what my body could conjure up when absorbing the increasing stress I was under. I started to notice that everything I ate — *anything* I ate — gave me a moment's relief from what had become a constant burning in my stomach. Even throwing back a beer at the Irish Pub seemed to briefly tamp down what I imagined was a vast acid pit. My symptom led me to an internist, then to a gastroenterologist, who told me I had an ulcer. He put my X-ray up on a screen and pointed out a small triangular area of my guts, saying my stomach looked like a 90-year-old woman's. I left with prescriptions to reduce the acid so the ulcer could heal, and some pink thing to drink before every meal.

Relentless optimism is not the same thing as truth, but since it had long been my habit to ignore anything that wasn't convenient, I took a perverse pride in this particular ailment. If I was going to work insanely hard and worry constantly about the future, I may as well have something to show for it.

≀

By the time the orchestra was a year old, I had gained more playing experience than during my four and a half years at school. (I'd also gained this hole in my stomach, but I could only guess that it had been brewing my last year and a half at Juilliard.) We played constantly. Stravinsky, Rimsky-Korsakov, Brahms, Berlioz, Glinka. Maxim Shostakovich came and conducted us through his father's Fifth Symphony. A Mozart festival. Another Florida tour. There was no other way to get this much experience. But all the experience and all the practicing wouldn't matter if there were no auditions. I had been in Miami for more than a year and there had been only one audition in that time. One audition that I hadn't even been allowed to take.

In May the orchestra had a break, and Doug and I decided we needed to buy cymbals. Because there were so many factors to consider in picking out a particular pair, we needed to visit the factory in Canada.

Sabian — the company that made these lumps of metal — had a long history. It began in 17th-century Turkey and ended with a family rift in the early 1980s that split the company in two. One brother seemed to be luckier than the other: he got to keep the Zildjian name — the most well-known cymbal brand among drummers — and got to live in Boston, while the other had to come up with a new name and was banished to Meductic, New Brunswick.

Doug met me at my parents' house in Rochester and we drove across New York State, through Vermont, New Hampshire, and Maine. We played Tracy Chapman's new tape and old Genesis recordings and talked. Doug had a girlfriend back in Cleveland and said they would get married, so we talked about the number of kids they would have — he wanted four but didn't know if she would agree to so few. His girlfriend was Catholic, so we talked about religion and abortion. She was also a singer, and I wondered how their raising kids would fit in with her career, but by now I knew that question was aggressive and rude and I didn't ask. Even on a drummer-bonding road trip, with all those hours in the car, we didn't talk about pressure, ulcers, Inderal, or auditions.

We pulled into New Brunswick after dark, and Doug saw nothing wrong with knocking on the door of a lonely farmhouse (I was thinking serial killers) to ask if we could camp on their vast lawn; the owner told us we could but had answered from the safety of an upstairs window (he'd apparently seen the same movies). We pitched a tent and slept under the endless Canadian sky. In the morning we drove to the factory.

There was scant beauty to be found in this part of the country — we passed no cliffs, waterfalls, oceans, lakes, or mountains — just flat land and a road. Meductic happened when the road veered left and made a crescent-shaped foray into a few houses and the cymbal factory. One of the workers actually voiced our feelings by admitting that during the winter there was an incredibly loyal workforce because they had nothing to distract them and were grateful for a place to go. Then he led us past the metal-melting ovens, the soundproof "hammering" room, where two men with industrial-strength hearing protection banged random small dents into the metal, and into a room with shelf upon shelf of stacked cymbals.

This was a candy shop for us; instead of going to a music store and trying out the pair or two that someone else had matched, we were able to make our own pairs from hundreds of cymbals. We decided on the size we wanted and the thickness, and then spent a few deafening hours picking out the one cymbal that had a nice ring, a good range of highs and lows, some splash but not too much, and then finding another equally good cymbal that sounded good when crashed against the first. When we'd narrowed down the choices, we took the pairs outside and played them for passersby on the Trans-Canada Highway. We'd been so deep for so long in our narrow orchestral percussion groove that I didn't consider the spectacle we made: two unwashed Americans, winding up and crashing cymbals by the side of the road.

ɀ

Back in Florida, New World was experiencing exponential growth. Raising money for touring was hard even for the most established orchestras in the country, but it didn't seem hard for New World. And after only 15 months in existence, we were leaving the country. In July, we played a concert in Paris, at the Bastille Opera House. In August, we went to South America. Starting in Buenos Aires, we played at the Teatro Colón, a concert hall famous for acoustics that rivaled Carnegie's. We went to Montevideo and São Paulo, playing huge repertoire like Beethoven and Bruckner symphonies, and Stravinsky's *Firebird*. Those of us with big instruments were remembering how hard it was to keep in shape while touring. Percussion and timpani, harp and basses all traveled in cargo trunks and were unloaded just before the concerts (by real crews — no duties for us on this trip). That meant we had to warm up and cram some practicing into the time between the sound check and the concert. We flew back to New York on August 12 and on August 13 played a concert at Wolf Trap outside of Washington, D.C.

We were then scheduled to have a month break until our Miami season started. I wanted to take an audition with the Pittsburgh Symphony, but they had looked at my meager résumé and asked me to send a tape. This they found lacking, though, and so instead of staying in Miami to practice for an audition, I went home to Rochester.

At this point in my life, when my main reason for getting out of bed in the morning was to practice for auditions, being excluded from those auditions was exasperating. It contributed some percentage to the acid bath in my stomach but it also made me mad. The only way to learn to take auditions was to take auditions.

One of the biggest advantages of living with other musicians was our mock auditions — the fake trials we set up to mimic the process in all its nauseating grandeur. If two or three of us were preparing, we'd gather a "committee," give them our list and let them pick a short list of excerpts, play a "prelim" round for them from behind a screen, then let them pick the "semifinalists." This was the best way to duplicate the warming up and the waiting. What was impossible to conjure was the terror and dread and anxiety, and the feeling of wanting to barf.

But getting excluded from auditions was also a gift. Cleveland hadn't invited me, nor Pittsburgh. The kind of practicing I did for an audition made me better at playing the excerpts but rarely led to any changes in technique or concept. The period between auditions was the time to risk taking a step backwards in order to take a greater leap forward.

As enjoyable as it was to perform and tour, it was important not to enjoy it too much. Just like at Juilliard, the point was to get out. New World would continue, but with a never-ending stream of conservatory graduates eager to come replace us in the Plymouth, our duty was to practice and get jobs. And it was starting to happen: one of the bassoon Johns had joined the Florida Orchestra in Tampa, and Amy had gotten a job in Jacksonville Symphony. And the reviewer in Tampa could now believe in Santa Claus: there had been an audition for principal horn in the Florida Orchestra and, despite the odds, Dave had won. For instruments that had frequent auditions, the turnover was ongoing.

The orchestra was also having an effect on Miami Beach. It now owned not only the Plymouth and the smaller hotel next door, the Ansonia, but earlier in the year had purchased a rundown art-deco movie theater on the Lincoln Road Mall, a five-minute walk from the Plymouth. Now we could continue our concerts in downtown Miami and then repeat them in our own hall on Miami Beach. The building also had several floors just for practice rooms. This reconstruction was the first big renovation of the mall — from Alton Road to Washington, it was originally designed as a pedestrian mall, but in the 18 months we'd been living there, it had only been a wasteland of algae-filled fountains, urine-filled doorways, and empty shops. With the arrival of the New World real estate juggernaut, it was showing signs of life.

After coming back from my month in Rochester and while the renovations to the Lincoln were taking place, we rehearsed in a choir loft in downtown Miami. This rehearsal period killed any remaining enthusiasm we had left for our crew job. With no elevator, we carried hundreds of pounds of timpani up two flights of narrow stairs. And on Saturdays, we carried them back down. Four timpani, one bass drum, bells, a xylophone, snare drums, trap tables. We decided to forfeit our extra $50 a week, and the orchestra hired professionals to replace us — men who were paid to wreck their arms, hands, and fingers moving our equipment.

⸘

We entertained the classical-music masses in Miami that second full season with new and bigger guest conductors than we'd had before: Neeme Järvi, Sergiu Comissiona, Christoph Eschenbach. Michael took us on two tours. The first included a concert in Carnegie. The *New York Times* made sure to contain any enthusiasm for what was a huge accomplishment for such a new orchestra. Although the critic mentioned that 33 of us had already won jobs, he went on to say, "The result was impressive in spots, a little shy of the big time in others." About the Beethoven Seventh Symphony, he said, "Except for a lively, driven final movement, it was pretty ordinary and — apart from a distinctive first oboe — the playing was ordinary, too, with weak and muddied interior lines and a thick, mushy texture over all." The critic was at least prescient about one musician's future. Within the year, that "distinctive first oboe" would win the biggest position in New World's short history: he became a member of the Boston Symphony.

It was possible to argue that my worldview had been drastically limited by being sheltered in such an insular world, but I could not imagine that a bigger thrill existed. After our oboe player won the job, I asked him what the audition had been like. For the final round, each of the two finalists played part of the Mozart concerto with the full orchestra. Standing on that stage, playing that first ascending scale, he said, felt like he was going up to heaven. In my fantasy, the ascension might be tempered by my anxiety, but the idea of playing in the finals for Boston was almost unimaginable. In my mind, other percussionists did that, older percussionists.

Our second outing was a four-city tour with the actress Audrey Hepburn. Michael had composed a piece for narrator and orchestra called *From the Diary of Anne*

Frank, which Hepburn would narrate. If it was a stretch to hear a 13-year-old's voice in Ms. Hepburn, she made up for it with her blindingly beautiful smile. She and her gorgeous, younger male companion traveled with us to Houston, Chicago, and Philly, before we ended the tour by playing at the United Nations General Assembly Hall in New York.

≀

With all of us living on an island and having so little exposure to anyone outside the orchestra, it was probably not a great surprise that some *Lord of the Flies* behavior began to emerge. During rehearsals and concerts, our savage selves were subdued. When there was a conductor on the podium, waving a stick at us and grunting from his throne, we acknowledged his supremacy. He stood, we sat. Back at the Plymouth, anarchy reigned. There were 90 leaders, some more sure than others that they should define the rules. Dating, mating, practicing, smoking, indoor cat privileges, recycling habits, hours of patio use, room assignments — all had to be decided. The methods were not always elegant.

I can imagine no other reason why James, Doug, and I saw fit to tell Laura, the fourth member of our section, that she might want to think about getting out of music. One day late in the spring, Laura was enjoying our day off in her room, blasting the Christian vocal group Take 6 from her tape player. She opened the door to us, smiling, completely unprepared, and within minutes of entering, Doug had taken the lead and told Laura we were there because we felt she wasn't committed to the orchestra. Realizing that James and I had abandoned him to deliver the news, he went on, saying she was divided in her loyalties, splitting her time between percussion and God, and we thought she needed to make a decision about where to put her energy. He even said she was taking a spot that a more committed drummer should have. Laura had been doing a minimum amount of practicing and wasn't performing up to our standards, so we wanted to kick her off the playground.

She cried. Then, instead of inviting us to kindly fuck ourselves, she said she would think about what we'd said and let us know. After a few days, she said she'd decided to quit pursuing music as a profession and was already looking into missionary work in Mexico for the summer. God, she said, had given her a sign and the sign was us — knocking on her door on a Sunday afternoon and giving her our unsolicited opinion.

Harsh reality, this. Aside from the fact that we were quite obnoxious in thinking it was our business to decide who should and shouldn't be in New World, we had a point. Laura hadn't been practicing, hadn't been anticipating the auditions we were hoping would come. She hadn't enthusiastically joined us at the rec center when we'd lined up all of our triangles and tambourines, trying to figure out what sounded best for which excerpt. There was no place here for a recreational drummer.

20
Boston

Finally — a real audition. The Boston Symphony was accepting résumés for an audition to be held in October. With James concentrating on timpani auditions now and Laura's spot not yet filled, Doug and I would be the only two New Worlders trying to get invited. But first we would have to pass a tape round.

We were lucky to have the new Lincoln Theatre. The Plymouth would never have the quiet time we needed. We were also lucky that the New World season was starting with a Beethoven festival. With few exceptions, Beethoven had written for timpani but not percussion, so while the rest of the orchestra was downstairs rehearsing onstage, Doug and I were upstairs in the unfinished construction zone. Soon these former offices would become practice rooms; for now the whole floor was filled with construction materials and demolition debris. Doug and I set up the short list of instruments we would need, then took turns recording. I joked to him that we should each record half the excerpt and splice them together. We barely let ourselves laugh. At Juilliard there had been a trombone player who sent off what was a spectacular example of trombone excerpt playing — unfortunately, it was his teacher's spectacular playing. He had somehow borrowed and copied the excerpts he needed and submitted them as his own. His idiocy was discovered when one of the listeners on the committee recognized the teacher's playing. Not something a musician could recover from. He left New York and music.

Boston accepted both of our tapes. Since we knew most everything about most everyone in the percussion world, we learned that they'd accepted very few. Some musicians were invited without a tape — those who already had jobs or whose playing was already known to the orchestra's percussion section. It would be a small audition, far smaller than the cattle calls I'd been to in the past. The advantage was that the committee might have slightly more listening time per person.

Then we got the list of excerpts.

It was the *War and Peace* of lists. Just reading through the five pages took several minutes; practicing that many excerpts would take all my waking hours until the audition. I had never seen a list remotely like it. It was not uncommon to have a solo piece on an audition — this list had five: two unaccompanied Bach solos on marimba, a ragtime xylophone piece, a four-mallet and a two-mallet solo of our choice. Then, excerpts on xylophone, bells, snare drum, tambourine, triangle, bass drum, cymbals, castanets, timpani, and even flexatone. *Flexatone*. A small rectangle of sheet metal, maybe six inches by two, attached to a wire frame, a wooden ball dangling on either side of the sheet metal. If you shook the whole contraption so the balls alternately struck the metal, all the while bending it with your thumb to raise and lower the pitch, it replicated the ghost sounds from *The Brady Bunch* when the kids were trying to scare away potential house buyers. There was actually a solo in the Khachatourian Piano Concerto for this instrument. Not just a random sound effect, though — it had actual pitches that went beyond the range of a single flexatone. Just learning this one excerpt involved buying two flexatones, a high and a low one, and rigging up homemade gauges out of cardboard so I could mark off the general area of each pitch. All of this before I even sat at the piano and actually learned the tune and then tried to replicate that on a piece of bent metal. And that was for the *least* important excerpt.

Because of the ongoing Beethoven festival, we had no obligations until the day of the preliminary audition. That is, no obligations except to practice until we hallucinated. I needed to start with mallets. Five solos, all of which had to be memorized. That was not required by the orchestra; most of us memorized solos in order to play them accurately. It was impossible to look at the music and the keyboard simultaneously. To save precious minutes of transit time, I turned my room at the Plymouth into a practice space. New World, with its vast and growing endowment and Yamaha sponsorship, had so many instruments Doug and I barely needed to share. I moved in a marimba and a xylophone, set up a snare drum, covered the surface of my dresser and kitchenette counter with tambourines and triangles. I taped the list to my wall. Down the hall, Doug and I set up an empty room with a vibraphone and bells. Bass drum and cymbals we could practice at the Lincoln. In the lobby of the Plymouth, there was an empty storage room we had long ago annexed as a timpani practice room.

I practiced like a factory worker punching the clock. Up at eight, I practiced until 11 — at night. With three hours a day for eating and showering, that still worked out to 12 hours a day of practicing. Most instrumentalists could not possibly do that — brass or woodwind players' lips couldn't take that amount of abuse, nor would they probably need to. But because we had so many different instruments, we both needed to and could. With so many different movements, we weren't as likely to cause ourselves repetitive motion injury.

For all the years of rivalry I'd had with Caroline and Sebastian, I had never felt the kind of competition I now felt with Doug. Caroline and Sebastian and I had competed for some vague future glory. This was Doug running in the lane next to me — practicing for the same job at the same time in the same space. If our quest had been a movie, the state of my stomach acid would be represented by a tea kettle screaming on the stove — for two months. I didn't know how he was dealing with it because we didn't talk about it. Still, we supported each other, sharing his favorite pair of marimba mallets and my favorite set of castanets, listening to each other play through our solos.

In the last weeks before the audition, the schedule began to take a toll on both of us. One night I went to talk to Doug and found him just hanging out with his girlfriend, not practicing. He was having arm problems and said he might have to skip the audition. Then it happened to me. I started noticing a biting pain in my right shoulder, deep in the socket. Panicking, I found the name of a physical therapist in Miami. He himself had been in constant pain after an accident and had to learn how to cure himself. He did some massage on me and taught me some exercises. Muscling through might have worked if it had only been a matter of ignoring the pain. But sore and swollen limbs were not terribly responsive limbs. I didn't practice any less, but I treated myself like a big superstitious baby, massaging my arm, exercising it, begging it for a few more good weeks. Somehow, both Doug and I managed to coax our weary limbs through the last few days of practicing and onto the plane.

It never occurred to me to travel with Doug, or anyone else, to an audition. Making only $300 a week, it would've been fiscally smart to double up, share cabs and maybe a hotel room. Supportive as we were of each other, though, this part of the journey was as solitary as if it were death itself. Maybe it was a tacit acknowledgment that at the end, there was only room for one.

During the ride from the airport, the cabbie asked where I was from, what I was doing there. When I said it was for a job interview, he asked if I would be willing to exchange the sun in Miami for snow, as if it were a regular job and the decision was mine to make. He was just making conversation, but not of a kind I understood. I would give up a city, a guy, weather, my soul — anything to have this job.

⟩

In the morning, I woke up and called Doug's hotel. He was scheduled to play in the morning group and I was in the afternoon. We had arranged to get together after his audition so he could give me the mallets and castanets we were sharing. Every orchestra had different procedures for informing the candidates if they'd moved on to the next round; some orchestras liked to tell the person right after they played, some liked to hear a group of five or ten and then announce who would continue. I knew when I heard Doug's hesitant voice that he'd been told he'd moved on. He didn't want to jinx me, but I asked him and he confirmed it. If I'd had room for any more pressure, I would have felt it then.

It had been two years since my last audition. When I walked out onstage I saw two rows of instruments and a partition the size of the Berlin Wall. Hidden behind the wall was the committee.

There was a remarkably loud buzzing going on in my head. I started playing Kreisler's *Tambourin Chinois* on xylophone. I was so wound up I played the accelerando at the end as if I were racing to a finish line. It sounded like a record spinning on the wrong speed. That is, what I could hear of it through all the buzzing. My hearing was so distorted it felt like an entirely different sense than I'd woken up with that morning. I moved to bells and played *The Magic Flute*. The bells had been positioned for a basketball player; they were so high, I stood on my toes and tried to concentrate on not falling over. They were also so shiny that the effect of the stage lights on them blinded me. That was at least three out of five senses messed with. Smell and taste could do me no good.

When I walked offstage, the personnel manager told me to come back in an hour. At that time they would tell us — the last group of the day — who had moved on to the semis.

I found the bathroom and went into a stall. I bawled from the release of pressure and from the strong conviction that my performance had not been good enough. For the next hour, I wandered the streets near the hall, trying to recall the audition. I didn't remember stopping in the middle of an excerpt, I couldn't think of any missed notes, I'd played with all the conviction I had, but it just wasn't perfect. I had a friend who brought his Walkman into auditions and taped himself; now I knew why. Whether from extreme focus or extreme distraction, I could barely remember what had happened. Heading back to the hall, I tried to convince myself that I would survive Doug surpassing me in this audition. Like all ideas that were too painful to contemplate, I didn't take it too far and imagine how I would feel if he actually got the job.

Then I dutifully marched back to the personnel manager's office and he told me I had moved on to the semifinals.

≀

Instead of forcing the committee to sit through two or three endless days of percussion excerpts, they separated the semifinals and finals from the prelims and paid for us to fly back. Within two weeks I was flying back to Boston for the second round. This time I knew I played well. While we waited for the rest of the semifinalists to play, Doug and I had lunch. Back in the hall, they told us there would be four finalists, including Doug and me.

Now I had to wait. The other semifinalists had packed up and gone home, and the four of us had drawn numbers to determine our order. I was last. The personnel manager said it would be awhile, but couldn't say how long. I guessed about when to warm up and for how long, when to take Inderal and how much. Then I waited some more. In the basement they had Wenger practice rooms, enclosed contraptions that were supposed to be sound-proof. I sat in one and could hear the faint sound of a xylophone bleeding through the many insulated layers. I put in earplugs.

Two hours and 15 minutes later, it was my turn. I walked onstage, this time to a crowd of musicians: the long-haired music director, the percussion section, other musicians on the committee. I put my snare drum in front of a music stand, laid out my mallets, and started to play.

If I could have conjured the perfect audition, this would have been it. I played the Bach partita, then the fugue, then the xylophone rag. Instead of feeling judged, I felt like I was showing off at a recital. The excerpts — first on xylophone, then bells, then snare drum — felt more like solo pieces than the absurd fragments they actually were. Even my timpani excerpts went as well as I could have hoped for. For 45 minutes, I just played. There was so much music they had asked us to prepare, I never even got to tambourine, cymbals, bass drum, or triangle, much less flexatone. Whatever Zen master had taken over my body was wishing she could have left them with a rousing rendition of the Khachatourian.

Then we waited. Doug and I and a third drummer sat together in a downstairs lounge. We talked about Leonard Bernstein, who'd died just the day before. The fourth drummer, Sam, wandered around like he couldn't bear to be still, then finally came and joined us. Waiting before and waiting after were two different kinds of torture — one because you could still influence the outcome and the other because you couldn't.

It was dinnertime by the time we had all finished playing, and even with the small amount of audition experience I had, I figured the committee was going to be desperate to finish deliberating and get out. They had heard more percussion in one day than they had bargained for. It wasn't long before the personnel manager came down the stairs.

He started by thanking us for coming. "You all played really well," he said, and took an agonizing few seconds to look meaningfully at each of us. "But today the job goes to Sam."

Sam was sitting next to me, and I looked at him in time to see his jaw drop. His eyes were wide, his mouth was a perfect "O" — his was the face of a person who, refusing to waste time on the aspects of the audition he couldn't control, had probably not imagined winning the job before this very moment. In an instant, his life had changed drastically.

There was praise for all of us. There were other staff members and some committee members who took the time to come down and talk to us, telling us we had all played well. Doug and I collected our many belongings and shuffled out of the hall. He seemed happy, taking our success as a good sign, that we had gotten this far and could do it again. If I had imagined this scenario back when I was in school, I would have thought I'd feel the same. There'd been a drummer at Juilliard who finished a few years before me and who'd gotten into the Chicago Symphony finals when he was still at school. Back then, I'd viewed that as a great accomplishment — I couldn't imagine how amazing it would feel to get to the finals of a major audition. But now I wondered why that audition was what we mentioned when we talked about this drummer. If he'd gone on to *win* an audition, wouldn't we be talking about that instead?

At the moment, I was in shock. And then, in shock at *being* in shock. Had I thought I was going to win? I couldn't understand why I was morose. I also couldn't have guessed that the way I was feeling was going to get much worse.

21
Losing It

I lost it.

"It" was my confidence, my desire to get up in the morning and practice, and the certainty that I would get a job.

Maybe if there had been a break, I would have been fine. My lack of practicing would have made sense after the huge effort of the last few months: time to concentrate on orchestra parts, time to let my shoulder heal. But there was no time to rest. Another big audition had already been announced, for the New York Philharmonic.

Suddenly I was faced with doing it all again. Tape, prelims, semis, finals. There was no building on this last audition, not in any concrete way. I should have felt great — in good shape from all the practicing I'd done, confident because I was playing at a competitive level. I should have felt like Doug. He was happy he'd done so well. He and his fiancée had decided they didn't want to live in New York, so he wouldn't be taking this audition.

But I wasn't thinking about having done well. I had

worked *that* hard and played *that* well and still lost. I felt like a colossal failure. Failure as in *failure*. Not my former Pollyanna definition of failure, which I could've summed up with the speech I gave myself: *I've just found another way that didn't work, it's a marathon not a sprint, failure is essential for success.* I'd always thought that having that attitude, along with being unafraid to fail, was a gift. Something I'd always known and hadn't had to learn. Now I knew there was such a thing: failure happened when you just stopped caring.

Richard wrote me a letter around this time. In it, he mentioned the New York audition. There was another drummer, Tyler, who was a frequent extra with the orchestra, someone Richard respected and liked. "I honestly don't know how I would feel if it came down to Tyler and Caroline," he wrote. At the time, I still intended to take the audition. He knew that. I didn't know in which way he was being passive-aggressive, just that he was. Was he saying he didn't think I would make it to the finals to compete with them? Or that, even if I did, he thought that they were the only two worth considering? Either way felt terrible.

After the tape deadline had come and gone, he wrote again: he could not believe I wasn't taking the audition. I could not afford to pass up rare opportunities like this. If I wanted to be an orchestral musician, I had to take every audition I could.

I could have gone, done well or badly, and no one would have cared or thought much about it. Auditions were by nature so arbitrary, the outcome depending on so many variables. I could get nowhere and my competitors would think whatever they liked — that I had a bad day, that Boston was a fluke, that I played great but the committee wasn't paying attention, that someone before me played so spectacularly that I looked weak by comparison, that I was bad, that I was great. Since I hadn't yet won anything, I still had nothing to lose. But the pressure I felt had never been external anyway. I had expected my personal upward trajectory of the past seven years to continue in a way that made sense. That meant the only logical step now was to win. It was the pressure I put on myself that was unbearable.

My room got messy. I didn't care enough to clean it. While I was practicing for the Boston audition, it had been filled with instruments; now the floor space was covered with dirty clothes. I let dishes sit in my sink until the silverware rusted. A little white mouse appeared from behind my bookcase one day: I had been sitting at my table so immobile he probably assumed I was one of the chairs. He darted away only when I screamed. One morning I went into the bathroom and saw — mercifully in a contactless blur — a palmetto bug laid out on its back in my tub. It looked like a cockroach from my New York nightmares (and reality) but one that had mutated in a radiation accident and was now three inches long. When I reached for it with a wad of paper towels, it flailed its many legs to show me just how alive it still was. It wasn't unusual for creatures to visit our unrefurbished dump in the tropics. It was unusual that I didn't care.

No one seeks out mental health care when they're happy. There has to be a good amount of pain or despair that shapes the will to make that phone call. When I first had an ulcer, the gastroenterologist suggested I see a shrink. I had called the first female psychiatrist I found in the phone book who was listed under auspices of the University of Miami. She turned out to be a Freudian who said "Ahh" when she thought I said something inter-esting. Having no experience with therapy and getting no direction from her, I guessed that my job was to entertain her. She gave me no hints that I should be telling her why I was overwhelmed or anxious enough to have called. We spent our fifth session talking about our experiences traveling to China, and then I quit, convinced that spend-ing those five hours practicing would have done more to alleviate my anxiety than talking to her.

I needed to try again. I spent so many years hiding my insecurities; admitting to another musician that I needed help felt like desperation. I *was* desperate. A friend who played in the orchestra in Fort Lauderdale recommended a doctor in Boca Raton. This new doctor was young enough and non-Freudian enough to know I needed help getting started. He asked questions and encouraged me to talk. He prodded me about my upbringing, which wasn't on my mind and didn't seem to be the problem, but was at least more relevant than the changing landscape in China. I started taking Prozac, the new miracle drug. I was trying.

The one place I didn't fall apart was in the orches-tra. That spring we played Prokofiev's *Romeo and Juliet*, Ravel's *L'Enfant et les Sortilèges*, Bernstein's *West Side Story*, Berlioz's *Symphonie Fantastique*, and I made the monumental effort to study the scores and practice the parts I had to play. I could not fail in rehearsals and per-formances. I desperately wanted to hang on to that last vestige of professionalism.

‰

Another audition came along, this time for the Cincinnati Symphony. It was the third major audition in six months. Once this position was filled, it wouldn't be open again for another 30 or 40 years.

I went through the motions. There was no tape round, so I sent in my résumé. I filled my room with instruments and started practicing the most common excerpts. When I got the list, I sat a chair in front of my file cabinet filled with its alphabetized folders and pulled out the music I needed. I called to find a flight, called to book a hotel room.

For two weeks I kept at it. I had always been a big fan of slow practicing — playing the excerpt perfectly before even considering speeding it up. Now I practiced slowly because I didn't feel like moving my arms faster. One morning I was playing my xylophone warm-up when I realized I couldn't think of any reason to continue. I went into my closet and closed the door. When I came out, I canceled my flight and my hotel room, called the orchestra and told them I would not be coming. The music stayed on the stands, the instruments stayed in my room. I walked around them.

It seemed unbearable to be living among so many musicians. I had them next door, above me, and across the hall. If I hadn't been on the ground floor, they would've been below. Anyone, anytime, could come by and hear I wasn't practicing. Worse, they could correctly assume I was in there doing nothing. I didn't have any hobbies: I didn't sit on the beach or exercise or windsurf. I took to walking along Collins Avenue at night, waiting until it was dark enough to see into other people's apartments so I could imagine living there and being someone else.

My other refuge was my closet. My room was too sunny, too exposed, and too big. There was a crack under the door that someone could peer under and scan the whole room, if that someone was willing to lie on the floor of the hall. When I closed the closet door and put in earplugs, I was alone.

Doug was practicing hard for the audition. I heard him every time I walked past his room. In rehearsals, he didn't waste a moment. Just before we started and during the break he practiced. When he was ready for a mock audition, I listened to him play the excerpts. One by one, he dispatched them with precision. He sounded like he was ready to win.

Over a period of a few days, I and the rest of the Plymouth followed Doug's progress through the audition. He played in the prelims and advanced to the semis. Then he advanced to the finals. Then he was playing in the finals with only three players. Moments after he called his fiancée, we all knew he had won. I saw Alicia in the lobby; she was ecstatic. In an instant, Doug and Alicia had a new life with security and a salary many times what he'd made for the past few years.

If Doug's success had happened at a time when I still only cared about excerpts, I would've been terrified. I would have taunted myself with the knowledge that Doug and I were in the same situation, had the same amount of practice time and the same access to all the instruments, yet he had won and I had lost. His success *was* a reminder that I was failing, but the feeling was muted. I cared about that no more than I cared about anything else. And somehow, the fact that I was more unnerved by missing the audition than I was by Doug's winning it took away a small amount of the pressure I felt about the competitors all around me. I was truly competing only with myself. Being in competition with Doug, or

Sebastian and Caroline or anyone else, was only about pushing each other to be better. When it came to the audition, I was alone behind that screen, giving my best effort. Everything else was beyond my control.

≀

Spring comes incrementally to Miami. In the northeast it's impossible to miss the change from snow to rain and then, abruptly, flowers. Here it was noticeable only in retrospect that the sun was brighter, even hotter, and the air conditioning was working harder.

Just as gradually, I started to care again. In May there was an audition for the San Francisco Symphony, and I went. In the prelims I played well and moved on; in the semis I didn't play well enough and didn't move on. I didn't feel like a failure for not living up to my self-imposed schedule for constant improvement — the relief I felt just going to the audition was tremendous. In my first three auditions — for the Met, Columbus, and Boston — I'd stayed in the prelims, advanced to the semis, then made the finals. In my mind, there was only one place to go after that. I think having a breakdown had been like hitting the reset button. I'd cut myself some slack and acknowledged that forward progress might involve a winding road.

≀

Since Bernstein's death the year before, Michael Tilson Thomas was now in charge of the Pacific Music Festival. The rest of New World was going back to Montana, but as conductor of both New World and Pacific, Michael had asked the drummers to spend a month with him in Japan and give a percussion ensemble concert.

Steve — who had replaced Laura in the orchestra — James, and I, planned a concert of hair-raising percussion classics. We wanted to give the Japanese audience the loudest, most American music we knew. The upper floors of the Lincoln were still unfinished, so we crammed our massive setups in and around empty doorways, the spaces between wall studs, and rooms whose ceilings were masses of exposed wires and plumbing. A drummer named Derek was the fourth in our quartet. He was headed back to PMF for his second year, so New World flew him down to rehearse with us.

Taking several cargo crates of instruments with us, we flew to Sapporo at the beginning of July. After the first week, our percussion concert was over and we were just members of the orchestra, attending the festival like the rest of the group. Unused to being students again, we balked at the master classes we had to attend. If they had been given by percussionists from American orchestras we would have gone happily, but they were given by members of the Vienna Philharmonic, who had an iconic style of playing — particularly the way they played waltzes. But once we picked their brains about that tradition, we weren't terribly interested in anything else they had to say.

In our few free hours, we wandered. Unlike Tokyo, there were few English speakers in Sapporo and we learned to add "o" to much of what we said. "Art Park" got us a quizzical look from a cab driver, but "Art-o Park-o" got us to the hall where we rehearsed. Some nights we walked to Susukino, Sapporo's downtown area, and marveled at what was peculiar to us — a Japanese businessman merrily taking a drunken piss on someone's chained bike — while the locals marveled at what was peculiar to them: Derek, the *gaijin* with the massive amount of chest hair sticking out of his collar.

In the second week of August, we flew back to Miami and to what was, for me, likely to be my last year in the orchestra.

22
I Believe

I had kept in touch with Richard since leaving school. He wrote long letters on his yellow lined paper, letters still full of his feelings for me. I wrote back short letters full of news about the orchestra: what we were playing, where we were traveling, who was conducting. When I first moved to Miami, he called occasionally, always on Sunday mornings. I did the same tap dance I'd done with him at our dinners — talk fast, only about music.

In 1990, I was in New York for a gig and had lunch with him. As we walked up Columbus Avenue, he commented that I'd gained weight. Patting my ass, he said I filled out my pants well now. I said nothing. At lunch, he mentioned that he'd heard I'd begun dating a clarinet player at New World and that we'd recently traveled to Maine together. Frowning, he said he could guess that it wasn't just a sightseeing trip. And then I told him: "I don't want to talk about anything like that anymore."

It wasn't sudden. It was time and distance. I was tired of smiling and pretending I wasn't uncomfortable.

Richard knew what I meant. Suddenly he was the one who shuffled and danced; he smiled, then got mock-serious, then seemed pouty, as if I'd scolded him. We walked back to school together. That night he came to the performance I played, and the next day I stopped by his studio. He began telling me how proud he was of me, and for a moment I thought he was talking about the fact that I'd told him I no longer wanted to discuss anything personal. I said as much.

"No," he said, frowning, "I wasn't happy about that." He meant he was proud of the way I played.

That day was the last time I saw Richard. And except for one final phone call, it was the last time I talked to him.

❧

On July 1, 1991, George H. W. Bush nominated federal Circuit Judge, Clarence Thomas, to succeed Thurgood Marshall on the Supreme Court. His confirmation seemed assured until a report of an FBI interview of Anita Hill was leaked to the press. In the report, Hill, a professor and Yale-educated lawyer, claimed that Thomas had sexually harassed her while she was his assistant at the department of Education and the Equal Employment Opportunity Commission. Hill was then subpoenaed to publicly testify at a Senate confirmation hearing for Justice Thomas.

According to Hill's testimony, Thomas had asked her out many times while employed by him. After she refused, she claimed, he used work situations to discuss details of his anatomy, spoke about women having sex with animals, and discussed pornography. Thomas vehemently denied the allegations.

In October 1991, I sat riveted as the hearings played out on TV. A composed Anita Hill told the country her story. Perhaps because of the many repetitions of this word on the news, it was the year "ha*RASS*ment" became "*HAR*assment." I watched as Republican senator Arlen Specter, gleeful and snickering and talking about pubic hairs on national TV, asked Anita repeatedly —*Why did she keep in contact with him after they no longer had to see each other every day? Why did she continue to work with him and follow him to a new job?* — and I thought, for the first time, maybe it's about power.

Like most Americans watching the hearings, I had always thought that sexual harassment was mostly about sex. Or at least touching or groping or fondling. And — absent the physical — it was just words and didn't amount to much. But harassment is about power. For me, it was about being unsavvy, being young, and wanting desperately to have a relationship with Richard. Just not the same relationship he wanted.

I could imagine being in Anita Hill's place. If there'd been a woman on the committee of 14, the questions might've been: *Did you want him to tell you he thought about you first thing in the morning and last thing at night? Did you want him to describe to you the physical effects of his blood pressure medication? Or did you just want him to teach you how to play?*

But there would only be Senator Arlen Specter. *So you went to dinner every week; did you ever tell him you didn't want to?* And Orrin Hatch, another Republican senator: *I have to say, if someone kissed me and I didn't want them to, I'd scream! How in God's name is he supposed to know you didn't like it if you didn't tell him so?* And most damning of all: *Didn't you actually date a teacher at Juilliard? Ms. Niemi — are you a fickle woman?*

Which always brought me back to this: no one had told Richard it was wrong. What was clear was that it wasn't clear.

The Clarence Thomas hearings were the beginning of a discussion that would go on for a long time. It still continues. The trial was supposed to be Thomas's but turned out really to be Anita Hill's. At the end of the trial, I realized why Anita and I and many others did our best to avoid thinking about it. Because at the end of the day, the committee didn't consider the fact that Thomas had power over Anita when they asked themselves the question *Why would a woman who was being harassed continue to stay in that man's orbit?* If they had, maybe they wouldn't have told Thomas what they ended up telling him: *Welcome to the club.*

23
Winning

For three and a half years — as long as the existence of the institution itself — I'd been safely embedded in the New World Symphony. The concession to those of us who'd been there since the beginning was that we could stay for a fourth year. I was on borrowed time.

After a banner year of auditions, it looked like there would be several more this year. Math was neither my training nor my strong point, but I made this calculation: by the end of next season I would have overstayed my official welcome by 12 months. I didn't spend one conscious moment on a backup plan — a backup plan meant planning for failure. The awareness was there anyway — walking by retail stores made my stomach acid pit lurch as I tried to push away the image of myself joining that workforce again. In line at Publix, I'd look away from the green smocks of the cashiers and their *scan scan bag, scan scan bag,* that hypnotic rhythm I knew too well from cashiering in high school, the only job for which I was trained.

Even with this awareness, I was calmer than I'd been before the events of the last year. I was still riding the pink cloud of gratitude, happy that my desire to practice had returned. I had no urge to examine my breakdown too closely, I just wanted to go and get a job.

꒰

The first audition that fall was for the Seattle Symphony. Seattle was unusual in the orchestral world; they'd undergone a restructuring and were no longer a part of the American Federation of Musicians. That meant they didn't have to adhere to any of the rules that governed audition behavior. From the start, they appeared to be going ahead with the usual routine — inviting all of us who sent in résumés, setting up a cattle call.

Two weeks before the audition I went to play for Matt in Fort Lauderdale. In going to him, I was traveling (at least a little) and playing on foreign instruments — two of the other variables that made auditioning hard. In falling apart the season before, I'd lost none of my anality. I continued to obsess about ways to control every detail of the process, trying to make the unpredictable more predictable.

When Steve or Brian (our replacement for Doug) and I played mock auditions, we dumped on each other. We were doing what we thought was best. No one knew the excerpts as well as we did, so we nitpicked each other to death, pointing out every miniscule flaw we heard. But Matt pulled a tactic on me that I didn't realize was a tactic: he made me think I was the greatest orchestral percussionist who had ever traversed a stage. He heaped praise on me — pointed, thoughtful praise — and instead of any criticisms, suggested different approaches I could consider.

Matt was older and he was a teacher as well as a performer. He knew that the best gift he could give me was confidence. He was more of a shrink than my shrink was a shrink. And he was my cheerleader, too.

I flew to Seattle feeling great. But in the spirit in which music is like a sporting event, I just did not have a good day. My hands were freezing and I couldn't warm them up. I didn't get out of the prelims. Another lesson learned, another note to self — *Make sure to pack gloves next time.*

I was still seeing my actual shrink and had an appointment with him when I got back. He wanted to talk all about the audition. I told him about the outcome and the rumor that accompanied it: that despite advertising it as a "real" audition, they had gone ahead and chosen the person who'd been playing extra with the orchestra even though (again, rumor had it) the only other candidate in the finals played so well that the stunned, embarrassed committee was forced to admit that the music director chose the extra because he felt obligated to. Even with landlines as our only tool of communication, these rumors were on the ground before the planes flew the finalists home.

I told the shrink that the only unusual part (if it was true) was that they had admitted it. We all complained about "rigged" auditions — any audition where it seemed they already had someone in mind, but for union reasons held an audition to give the appearance of propriety. The truth was, we could never know the truth. That chosen person may have been the best player that day. Sometimes a "rigged" audition was any audition that the complainer had not won. There wasn't a good solution: Baltimore had put a job announcement in *International Musician* two years before; after accepting our résumés, they retracted it and sent a letter explaining that they were canceling the audition because they had decided to hire their long-term substitute. Even though they'd chosen to be upfront, we complained about that, too. But the point was, complain and then move on. Spending too much time talking about it meant I would be dwelling on something I couldn't control instead of just practicing.

But the purpose of therapy is to dwell. The shrink then wanted to know how I felt about not winning the job. I said I had learned from the audition and now — on to the next. But didn't I want to analyze my feelings on the subject? Pointless, I said. I needed to analyze my loud snare-drum roll. To analyze my feelings about a process that offered difficult odds, even when it functioned perfectly, would serve no purpose for me.

Having pushed me as much as he could, he finally gave me an "All right" and a coy smile and said, "You seem to have worked this out." Clearly, he thought I needed to denounce the profession entirely. I could have my cathartic cry in his office, rage against the iniquities of the music industry, and then run to Eckerd's and fill out an application to work at the pharmacy counter.

Instead, I quit therapy. The biggest lesson I'd learned from the past year was that one audition, no matter how heartbreaking, didn't matter. Auditioning was a process, and potholes were not a departure from that journey, but a part of it.

{

During that fall there was rumbling within some quarters of the orchestra about organizing ourselves to better our conditions. One oboe player's favorite saying eloquently summed up the feeling: *They're fucking us up the ASS.* While not technically true, I could see her point. Our pay was low, we had no control over our schedule, no security about how long we could stay. I was of two minds and two faces about the issue — happy to bitch loudly with my peers, completely unwilling to spend time organizing or sticking my neck out. New World had never claimed to be a job, and for us to pretend otherwise when we were so eminently replaceable was stupid. I wasn't secure enough to spew treacly sentiment and risk peer disapproval, but I still thought we were lucky to be there. Outlook still influenced by my Prozac glow, I was also just out for myself. I didn't need to think about improving New World, because the orchestra was doing spectacularly well on its own.

In December and January, we went on two more tours. Ten days in Japan playing Copland and Brahms, ten days in Scotland and England playing Ives and Gershwin. At the Barbican Centre in England, we played a percussion ensemble concert in the lobby just before the orchestra concert. For the first time since playing "Frivolity" at Juilliard, I played a xylophone rag in a concert. The part of the performance that involved my hands went well; north of there — in my brain — I had a more disturbing experience. The rag, called "Whirlwind," was an impressive showpiece and ended with such a flurry of notes that the audience couldn't help but erupt into loud applause. As I bowed, my unsettled brain was wondering if the applause was really worth it. I was tabulating the stress I had felt preparing for the concert. Part of the stress involved playing it on tour — it took far more effort to get practice time on the instrument when we were traveling. But I also wondered if playing from memory wasn't the next logical thing to get hysterical about. It made sense — even if my hands were in no danger of shaking, Inderal did nothing to keep me from having a memory slip. I had the feeling, sometimes, that I was racing to get a job before my nerves overwhelmed me.

✯

In the spring, audition number two for the year: the Indianapolis Symphony.

I flew to Indianapolis, staying in a hotel in the tiny downtown area. Since I was already practicing as much as possible, my goal now was to refine the audition-taking skills that were outside the playing realm. To an outsider I would certainly look caught in the grip of an OCD tailspin: I decided to write out an Inderal chart so I would know how much and when I had taken each dose; I brought a portable wooden box to stand on because they had sent out the vertical measurement of the bells and they were too tall for me to play comfortably without a boost; I thought of amusical topics to talk to my competitors about — family, hometowns, dogs — anything to keep us from discussing stick choices or snare drums. After the experience in Seattle, I remembered to keep my hands warm. To keep the process moving and save time, we usually waited just outside the stage door for the person in front of us to play, so I brought along earplugs. I didn't want to hear that person play well, which would make me nervous, or hear the person fall apart and play badly, which would also make me nervous.

The first round went well — I even earned a "Great" from behind the screen after playing the *Capriccio Espagnol* excerpt. That was the same snare-drum part that had been my undoing in Westchester nearly eight years before. I moved on to the semis. In that round I started with timpani, played snare drum and bells, and then moved over to xylophone, where there was an unfamiliar piece of music sitting on the music stand. Whatever blood had been circulating in the area of my face quickly drained. Although I'd never encountered it before, the possibility that the committee would deal out a piece of music not on the list was fair game. I wasn't unprepared for the fact of sight-reading, I was struck dumb by what looked to be the highest proportion of black to white I'd ever encountered on a page of music. It looked like the paper had gone through a copier and there'd been an ink accident. The personnel manager said I had a minute to look it over — he timed it with a stopwatch — and then, through some combination of luck and enough laserlike focus to burn a hole in the page, I played it well. Not perfectly, but I earned another "Great" from behind the screen.

I knew, just like I'd known in Boston, that I'd made the finals.

I was wrong. When the personnel manager came into the waiting room and announced the name of the two finalists, there was silence. So much silence, in fact, that the manager seemed to feel the need to fill it, and kept talking, saying we should support our colleagues who had moved on, go and get them something to eat because they would have to immediately play again for the final round and wouldn't have time to go out themselves.

I was floored. It was true that my memory of playing

a great audition was entirely self-reportage, and trying to remember what happened during moments of extreme duress might not have prompted the most accurate recall. But the only recall I had told me I had played great. I spent the rest of the night in my hotel room and in the morning took a cab to the airport. I heaped scorn on the dump as I left. I wasn't going to live in India-no-place, with its nonexistent downtown and freezing cold weather and provincial ways. By the time I was back in Miami, I'd heard they'd put off making the decision about a winner by asking each of the two finalists to play with the orchestra at some future date.

⁂

At the end of March, New World played a concert with the Cuban-American pop star Gloria Estefan. She had somehow been persuaded to end her *Into the Light* tour with a benefit concert, and we would be her cover band.

From the first rehearsal, the orchestra was smitten with her. She was funny, beautiful, gracious, and humble. She gamely ventured into our repertoire, learning one of the *Carmen* arias by ear because she didn't read music. She and her band were utterly kind as we tried to unleash our uptight ways on her music. The percussionist encouraged and applauded us, and let us merrily pretend to play congas and bongos even as he probably had them turn the sound down on our microphones.

Univision, the Spanish-language network, recorded our concert at the Miami Arena before a crowd of 13,000. For the first half we tried the crowd's patience mightily, playing symphonic works that were as Latin as an orchestra could muster — Alberto Ginastera, Silvestre

Revueltas, Carlos Chávez — and then Gloria took over and captivated the audience. She came out in a glamorous gown, and I gawked shamelessly, trying to see if the low-cut back revealed any hideous scars from her tour-bus accident. Nothing — she was flawless. When she walked in front of the drummers, we screamed, "We're not worthy!" above the pandemonium, to which she laughed and screamed back, "Not!" It was an evening of pure musical joy, a departure from the scrutiny we usually felt at concerts. There was no pressure or exposure; we were just playing for fun.

꒰

The opposite of playing for fun was recording a CD. There was nothing like putting your playing down in permanent binary form to make your teeth clench long enough to grind your molars down to nubs. For our first attempt, we were recording music of Latin America: Ginastera, Chávez, Revueltas, and Astor Piazzolla. We were lucky. We were technically good enough to produce a great recording, but since we were not a professional orchestra we had more time to rehearse and the luxury of more time in the studio. The result was spectacular.

While we were recording, practicing, playing concerts, and gradually winding up another season, we were also packing up the Plymouth. New World had decided that the hotel needed a complete overhaul, which would take most of the next season. They needed to replace the aging window air conditioners that inefficiently dispelled the swamp air at an astonishing cost, replace the kitchen appliances, debug, repaint, recarpet. There were only six musicians left, including myself, who had joined

New World at the beginning and were still stalking the Plymouth's halls. I was living in the best room in the hotel. There was no escaping the bug issues or the stained carpet, but I now had my own private balcony — just in time to pack again and vacate in advance of the gutting of the hotel. The musicians would ride out the year scattered among the far skankier temporary hotels in the area. Since nobody had talked to me about leaving, I began packing my belongings for storage, along with the rest of the orchestra. I didn't want to ask about my status; I was hoping that not being told to leave was the same as being allowed to stay.

Before they locked the doors of the Plymouth and we scattered for the summer, there was one more percussion audition to take. Scheduled for the end of May, it was for the San Francisco Opera Orchestra.

Most of the New Worlders had already left. Those who were coming back had packed their boxes and left them stacked in their rooms. Those who weren't coming back packed a little more carefully and shipped their boxes to wherever they were headed next. Steve, Brian, and I were all taking the audition, and for the month of May had the luxury of living like the hotel belonged to us alone.

Just like the first audition I'd taken, for the Met, the list was small. Just 19 excerpts, no timpani. The three of us helped each other out. We shared albums from our trips to the library — there were operas like Shostakovich's *Lady Macbeth of Mtsensk* and Prokofiev's *War and Peace* that we were unfamiliar with and had to study. I practiced through the morning and early afternoon, then sometime near the end of the day, I recorded the excerpts. At night I would listen to the playback, pushing the headphones against my ears to hear over the hiss of the tape and the gushing of the dying air conditioner. After I was done for the day, I packed. Anything not essential went first — books, clothes, plates, glasses, and silverware collected over the years, old programs, the instruments and sticks and music I didn't need for the audition. At the last minute, my stereo. Finally, my snare drum, mallets, cymbals, and tambourine for the audition.

{

As we gathered in a basement rehearsal room on the morning of the prelims, I saw many familiar faces. With so many auditions over the past two years, we drummers now knew each other not just from school and festivals, but also from hanging out in rooms like this. We looked like well-dressed homeless people, trailing luggage carts with our belongings. I looked at the faces. Once again, someone in this room would win the prize. Everyone else would go home.

Throughout that weekend they whittled our numbers down. By Sunday afternoon, there were four finalists: a freelancer who lived in the area, Steve, Brian, and me.

For only the second time, I faced a committee without a screen. About ten musicians were seated at a long table. The table was covered with paper, pencils, and coffee cups. I stood in front of the xylophone in my gray pants and black turtleneck, an audition outfit carefully chosen to look professional and neutral, nothing flashy, no loose material or dangling sleeves to get in the way. I wore flat, rubber-soled shoes so I couldn't slip, and my big bug glasses so I wouldn't have to deal with a contact gone astray. Nothing left to do but play.

I played first; now I was the one who had to wait for the others to finish. I paced in the hallway, walked up and down the stairs, drank at the water fountain, went to the bathroom. I hummed to myself, loudly, to avoid overhearing any of the other three auditions. I stood at the glass exit doors and watched the traffic go by. Fog came in and the sun disappeared. When all four of us had finished, we waited together. I remembered the Boston audition, where Sam had separated himself from the rest of us during this waiting period. Suddenly superstitious, I walked outside, went to the corner, and came back.

The personnel manager had told us it wouldn't be long. I tried to imagine the committee's discussion. It wasn't hard — when Steve and Brian had joined New World, James and I were on the committees that chose them. We were the ones on the other side of the screen, we heard their excerpts, debated their merits, voted on a winner. Orchestras had different procedures — a straw vote, a discussion, a binding vote. Everyone on the committee had a voice. Then it was usually up to the music director to make the final decision. For one of the four of us, this was a time suspended between a life that had been and a life that would be. We just didn't know yet whose life it was that would change.

Finally, the personnel manager came into the room. He smiled at each of us, telling us that we had all played great. He thanked us for coming.

And then he said I was the winner.

To imagine winning before it happened would have been a distraction from the work it took to get there. So even though that was the goal through all those hours and years of practicing, it was impossible to picture that moment. It came as a complete surprise.

❧

I cried all the way back to New York. Starting in the cab on the way to the airport, I bawled through the long overnight flight. Giving up on the idea of sleep somewhere around the Great Lakes, I stared at the city lights of Chicago, watched how they abruptly stopped at the black curve of Lake Michigan. I was flying overnight because I had a rehearsal in the morning at Juilliard. During my years at school, I had played in the orchestra for the School of American Ballet's annual showcase; when it didn't conflict with New World, I kept playing it.

I was crying because so much had just changed. I wasn't going to live in Miami anymore. I was leaving New World, leaving the friends I knew. I cried because I knew that no matter what goal I set for myself in the future, it wouldn't be a journey as intense as this had been. Mostly I was crying because I was finally able to give in to thinking about how hard it really was to win an audition. It was like being stuck in a hurricane — all your energy goes toward just riding it out and surviving. It's not until you're rescued that you can finally allow yourself to give in to the fear that you might not have made it.

Of course, I still had to get tenure. This job was not guaranteed for me until I passed that hurdle. But somewhere over Pennsylvania, I had the first of many happy thoughts. My starting salary was going to be five times more than I was currently making. I would never have to work at a retail job again. As far as I knew, San Francisco didn't have palmetto bugs. I was actually going to live in a big, interesting city and, unless I chose to, I wouldn't have to live next to another musician.

Most of all, I would never work a day in my life. I only had to face the music and play.

Coda

New York is both a place and a time, and to say I lived there 30 years ago is to say to those who live there now: we never lived in the same town. Their Lincoln Center is anchored by a Century 21 store that stretches across 66th Street from Broadway to Columbus. Century 21 replaced John's Coffee Shop, with its blue-and-white coffee cups, and Bank Leumi, whose ATM dispensed $5 bills. Now, within blocks of Century 21 they have an IMAX, a Pottery Barn, and a Starbucks, everything they need to turn the Upper West Side into the Upper East. Below street level on 67th there was a typewriter repair shop that doubled as a copy shop; I would take music there and they would copy and bind it for me. At the bottom of the stairs, just outside the shop's door, was a pay phone. Now pay phones, copy shops, and typewriters are all a thing of the past.

Across from Century 21, there is still a triangle-shaped park. In the '80s, a man in a tweed suit presided over the park. He would ask passersby if they could "spare a token or a dollar for *trahns*port." Those are gone, too: the man, the dollar subway ride, and the token. Across Broadway, facing the park, Juilliard looks different. The facades of the school and Alice Tully Hall have been transformed. All of Lincoln Center has been erased and redrawn.

Inside Juilliard it's the same and it's different. Practice and practice more — but now all those percussionists inside the school and every other conservatory have fewer places to audition. The orchestras at the top are still there, but some orchestras in small and midsized towns have gone out of business.

In the directory of all U.S. orchestras, there are currently nine women among the 181 percussion/timpani players. In most ways, it means as much or as little as it did then. We audition behind a screen and play great or badly. The only control we have is to practice. The odds are worse, but for those who have the drive and the stamina, the prize is still there.

꠶

In 2014, I went to the theater to see *Anita*, a film that included many excerpts from the original Clarence Thomas hearings. In those excerpts, the message from the senators was: we don't believe it happened. But if it did happen, why *didn't* you speak up? And then regarding the trial, why *did* you speak up? *Are you a scorned woman?* After the film, Anita Hill herself spoke to the audience in the cinema. Those in power don't leave the situation, she said — we leave. Leave a job, leave school.

After the show I went into the alley to meet her. She was warm and gracious but in a hurry; her car was blocking other cars and her driver was telling her they had to go. She climbed into her car and I walked to the end of the alley and suddenly just started bawling. Since this was San Francisco and you can howl on the sidewalk and not attract attention, no one paid me any mind until her car reached the end of the alley and stopped in front of me. She rolled down her window, and I said, "You made me stop doubting myself." It sounds overly dramatic, but it was genuine. I had spent many years thinking I should've known how to deal with the situation with Richard, that the toll it took on me was my fault because I didn't leave Juilliard sooner.

The last time I talked to Richard was two days after I'd won the job in San Francisco. I was nervous because we hadn't talked in years, but the last disastrous time I failed to tell him about winning an audition (for New World) was still on my mind. So I told him I'd won a job and I told him where and what orchestra it was. His response: "Better you than me." To be fair, he was probably just voicing what was a bias against opera among some percussionists. Many drummers felt that playing percussion for an opera orchestra wasn't as thrilling as playing in a symphony because we were in a pit instead of onstage. But I had hoped he would say, "Congratulations."

I don't know what it's like for students now behind those closed doors. All colleges have sexual harassment seminars and workshops and handbooks. Richard did not have the benefit of these discussions and neither did I. What made a difference for me was hearing from Anita Hill. In the end — as she said at the presentation — all you can do is tell your story.

٢

Miami Beach has changed even more dramatically than New York City. If those of us arriving in Florida in 1988 had looked around at the war zone and thought of investing in real estate, we would've done well. What we saw on Collins Avenue — cats, dirt, drugs, porches with rocking chairs, a few hookers — turned into South Beach. It still had drugs and hookers, but of a much higher quality.

The New World Symphony has been wildly successful at attracting talent and fostering it. It's harder to get into the orchestra now than it is to get into some full-time jobs. New World was spectacular at preparing me for a real job. You get good at what you do, and for those four-plus years in Miami I played music in an orchestra. I arrived at my job in the San Francisco Opera already knowing that complimenting my colleagues would be good, but telling them what I would do differently would not be helpful; that the only real answer to a conductor's question is "Yes"; that being paranoid about playing *behind* the rest of the orchestra doesn't mean I should compensate by playing *ahead*. There was much I would need to learn that was specific to opera — like accompanying singers and playing in a crowded pit.

I still suffer from performance anxiety. From the time we first pick up an instrument, we musicians are scrutinized by teachers and compared to colleagues. We're subjected to auditions in which many of us compete for one position. Those of us lucky enough to win orchestra jobs find ourselves judged by audiences, reviewers, and conductors, a few of whom — while not lawsuit-horrible like J. K. Simmons's character in the 2014 film *Whiplash* — think nothing of belittling or demeaning those under their baton. We subject ourselves to this process because we are passionate about music and want to excel at creating it.

At some point in our careers, however, each of us must acknowledge the anxiety that comes from constant judgment. I've known a few musicians who appear to handle it effortlessly — feel the fear and do it anyway. My performance anxiety, which came on like a train, has not gotten much better over the past 24 years of my career. Therapy (various kinds) and medication (ditto) have helped me, yet done little to make it go away. Performing live is stressful: even if you have food poisoning and need to leave the pit and barf (happened), you still come back for the rest of the performance, because when the guy with the stick points at you, your job is to play.

Most people are deeply anxious about being judged. For some, repeated exposure helps, the way that getting small doses in the form of allergy shots can keep you from going into anaphylactic shock at the sight of a peanut. That hasn't worked for me. I've come away from decades of performing with an exquisitely heightened sensitivity to criticism. I still take Inderal for an especially big performance. I know many other musicians who have used it; I know some who haven't. I can only say this: I wish I didn't have the extreme anxiety that makes me feel it is necessary.

When I was at Juilliard, I couldn't imagine how musicians gave up before they'd climbed as high as they could on the orchestral food chain. Despite my love for my new position in San Francisco, there were many percussion jobs that were higher-profile. I still felt the competitive pull. In 1996, there was another audition for the Metropolitan Opera Orchestra. I started in with the familiar routine: practicing, listening to the excerpts, recording myself. Then, with the audition still six weeks away, I started to go crazy. I couldn't sleep. I stopped eating and lost ten pounds. For a few days I took up running because the anxiety made me feel like my body was constantly vibrating and I wanted it to stop. I wanted to cry all the time but wouldn't, because that would mean admitting something was very wrong. That kind of anxiety was one Inderal couldn't touch. I didn't take the audition — climbing any higher would only come with an anxiety level I couldn't imagine dealing with. I was lucky to win an audition for a job that I've now been happy with for 24 years.

It's not possible to avoid being judged — sometimes, our harshest critic is the face in the selfie. The difference now is I'd rather talk about performance anxiety. I look back at the student I was, pretending to muscle through unaffected by nerves, and wish I would have opened up to someone. Sharing our stories with each other is a gift, one that makes us realize we're not alone.

For while we practice alone, audition alone, obsess and worry alone, the beauty of an orchestra is how everything comes together. One of my favorite pieces of music to play now is Arrigo Boito's *Mefistofele*. The last five minutes of the opera have strings, winds, brass, percussion, playing; a full chorus, arms stretched to heaven, singing; the very Devil himself, onstage howling. It's a privilege that we get paid to do this job: every one of us making as much of that joyful noise, together, as is possible. It's a perfect ending.

Acknowledgments

It's true that few parents would pray for a drummer but I won the lottery by having two who could not have been more delighted. It simply would not have happened without them willingly giving vast amounts of time, money, energy, and some hearing to help me. To them and to the family they gave me — Nancy, Jen, and Julie — and the family I acquired — Chris, Tom, Heather, Gwen, Abigail, and Emily — thank you for everything.

To Malaga Baldi, my agent — my most heartfelt thank you. What a pleasure it's been getting to know you and work with you.

To the tremendously talented, enthusiastic, and patient team of book midwives at ECW Press — Jack David, David Caron, Erin Creasey, Crissy Calhoun, Stuart Ross, Jennifer Knoch, Laura Pastore, Susannah Ames, Samantha Dobson and the many I've not yet met — thank you for the care and hard work you give to what you do.

And to Bruce Musgrave, former Brighton High School English teacher — thank you and keep sharing your passion for reading and writing.

Published by ECW Press
665 Gerrard Street East, Toronto, ON M4M 1Y2
416-694-3348 / info@ecwpress.com

With the exception of recognizable public figures, all names have been changed
in order to protect the privacy of others. The events have been related from the author's
memory of these experiences.

LIBRARY AND ARCHIVES CANADA CATALOGUING IN PUBLICATION

Niemi, Patti, author
Sticking it out: from Juilliard to the orchestra pit, a percussionist's memoir / Patti Niemi.

Issued in print and electronic formats.
ISBN 978-1-77041-273-6
ISBN 978-1-77090-848-2 (pdf); ISBN 978-1-77090-849-9 (epub)

1. Niemi, Patti. 2. Percussionists—United States—Biography.
3. Orchestral musicians—United States—Biography. I. Title.

ML419.N672A3 2016   786.8092   C2015-907286-7
                                             C2015-907287-5

Cover design: Michel Vrana
Cover image: © erdemerdemli/iStockphoto
Author photo: John F. Martin
Type: Rachel Ironstone

Printed and bound in Canada by Friesens
  5   4   3   2   1

FSC
www.fsc.org
MIX
Paper from
responsible sources
FSC® C016245

Get the eBook FREE!